A GRAPHIC LIFE
OF
JESUS THE CHRIST

By
Rev. Albert Joseph Mary Shamon

Published for
THE RIEHLE FOUNDATION
by
FAITH PUBLISHING COMPANY
P.O. Box 237
Milford, OH 45150-0237

Nihil Obstat: Rev. Benedict A. Ehmann
October 21, 1994
Rochester, NY
Censor

The *Nihil Obstat* and *Imprimatur* are a declaration that a book or pamphlet is to be considered to be free from doctrinal or moral error. It is not implied that those who have granted the *Nihil Obstat* and *Imprimatur* agree with the contents, opinions, or statements expressed.

Imprimatur: ✠ Matthew H. Clark
Bishop of Rochester, NY
October 21, 1994

Additional copies of this book may be acquired by contacting:

For book stores: Faith Publishing Company
P.O. Box 237
Milford, OH USA 45150-0237
Phone: 1-513-576-6400
Fax: 1-513-576-0022

For individuals: The Riehle Foundation
P.O. Box 7
Milford, OH USA 45150-0007
Phone: 1-513-576-0032
Fax: 1-513-576-0022

MARY,

I HOPE WE BOTH ENJOY THIS
BOOK ABOUT THE LIFE OF JESUS.
BLESSED CHRISTMAS 1997

I LOVE YOU,

alf

I wish to thank Harvey Simmons III, Esq., of Skaneateles, New York and Mrs. Richard Funk of Oswego, New York, who read the manuscript and offered very helpful suggestions.

Contents

Page

Preface. vii
Introduction ix
Beginnings xiii

Part I: The Founding of the Kingdom—the Church

Chapter 1
    Beginning of the Public Ministry of Jesus 3
Chapter 2
    Hints Regarding the Nature of His Kingdom 13
Chapter 3
    Launching the Kingdom in Galilee 20
Chapter 4
    Building the Kingdom 31
Chapter 5
    Training the Twelve 51
Chapter 6
    The Parables of the Kingdom. 58
Chapter 7
    Jesus Promises a Head for the Kingdom 74

Part II: The Redemption

Chapter 8
    Winding Down the Galilean Ministry. 87
Chapter 9
    Feast of Tabernacles—the Judean Ministry 93
Chapter 10
    Feast of Dedication—the Perean Ministry 107

Chapter 11
    Final Ministry in Jerusalem (Holy Week). 122
Chapter 12
    Maundy Thursday 133
Chapter 13
    Good Friday. 143
Chapter 14
    The Crucifixion and Death of Jesus 162
Chapter 15
    The Resurrection of Jesus 176
Appendix: Chronology of the Life of Jesus 187

Preface

His public life was only two and one half years. No man ever did so much in so little time. It was a miracle!

He never left His homeland, yet He has touched the whole world.

He never went to the universities of the world, yet taught more than all the philosophers and professors of the world together.

He never wrote a book, yet no library in the world can contain the books written about Him.

He had nowhere on which to lay His head, yet He has won the hearts and minds of millions.

He healed the multitudes without medicine and made no charge for His services.

He drove out demons with a word—no spells, no incantations—because His kingdom was spiritual.

He was the salt of the earth, the light of the world, the leaven of mankind, and the Good Shepherd of all.

He said He was the way, the truth and the life (*Jn.* 14:6). He is the way to life eternal, because He is the truth. St. Paul told the jailer in Philippi, *"Believe in him . . . and be saved"* (*Acts* 16:31).

Introduction

The two eyes of true history are geography and chronology. To understand the events of history, it is imperative to know where and when they occurred.

For years, I simply read the Gospels. The incidents were indeed meat for meditation and inspiration. Yet, the full richness of these events was lost because I was unaware of their context. It was like looking at a diamond without its setting or the painting of a cathedral minus the landscape.

So it is worthwhile to study the incidents of the Gospels with their geography and chronology in mind, to see the whole picture! Hence this graphic life of Jesus the Christ.

Why did God choose the Holy Land for His Son's earthly mission? It was because the Holy Land at that time was the geographical center of the then known world. It would be relatively easy to carry the Gospel from there to the four corners of the earth. And that was precisely what the apostles did. Before the last one had died, the words of the Psalmist were fulfilled: *"Through all the earth their voice resounds, and to the ends of the world their message"* (*Ps.* 19:5).

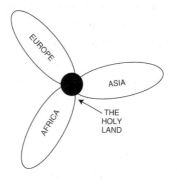

Why did God send His Son to earth 2,000 years ago?
He did this because it was in the "fullness of time." *"In the fullness of time, God sent His Son, born of a woman, born under the law," (Gal. 4:4).* The "fullness of time" meant that moment in history when all of mankind was looking for a religion that would answer all the questions of the mind and satisfy all the longings of the human heart.

Man has always needed religion because God created man in His image and likeness. As Augustine wrote: "For Thyself Thou has created us, O Lord, and our hearts are restless till they rest in Thee." Thus from the very beginning, man had devised some kind of religion.

But unaided by revelation, all he could concoct was mythology. Man's religions were myths. For a while they satisfied. But then they proved inadequate, so man would search for another religion. This new religion would serve him well for a time, but again its shortcomings would eventually surface. So man went from religion to religion until at the time of Jesus, man was apparently totally confused with all non-revealed religions.

He sought for one that had the fullness of truth, that could answer all his questions about life and satisfy all the yearnings of his heart. Thus pagans were turning more and more to Judaism. But even that did not fully satisfy them, for Judaism was but the foreshadowing of the religion that was to come with Jesus. Because Jesus brought the fullness of truth, His religion spread like wildfire. Within three centuries the Roman Empire became Christian.

A similar yearning on the part of C. S. Lewis brought him from atheism to Christianity. He wrote:
"The question was no longer to find the one simply true religion among a thousand religions

simply false. It was rather, 'Where has religion reached its true maturity? Where, if anywhere, have the hints of all Paganism been fulfilled?' . . . Paganism has been only the childhood of religion, or a prophetic dream. Where was the thing full grown?" (*Surprised by Joy,* pp. 187-8).

Lewis discovered the answer was in the Christian religion. *"In times past, God spoke in partial and various ways to our ancestors through the prophets; in these last days, he spoke to us through a son . . ."* (*Heb.* 1:1). And His Son said that He was "the way, the truth and the life." The way to life, because He was the truth—the fullness of truth!

* * *

The objective of Jesus' life was twofold: (1) to redeem the world by His passion, death and resurrection; and (2) to found a Church to bring His redemption to all peoples of all times and places.

Jesus began with the second objective first.

Founding the Church (His kingdom)— Galilean ministry

John the Baptist announced the kingdom.

Jesus laid the foundation of the kingdom by calling some of John's disciples.

Jesus explained the nature of His kingdom in the Sermon on the Mount.

By parables, Jesus showed that His kingdom would be ultimately victorious. And by exercising His miraculous powers He showed why it would be victorious.

The decisive test for membership in the kingdom was the Holy Eucharist—*"Do you also want to leave?"* (*Jn.* 6:67). Jesus promised to give His kingdom unity by promising to make Peter His successor and the visible head of the kingdom.

The Redemption—Judean ministry

Judean ministry: from Tabernacles, October, to December, Dedication, December, A.D. 29.

Perean ministry: from the Feast of Dedication, December A.D. 29, to His triumphal entry into Jerusalem (Palm Sunday), April 1, A.D. 30.

Last week in Jerusalem: from the Sunday of His triumphal entry into Jerusalem, April 2, to Saturday, April 7, A.D. 30.

The Resurrection of Jesus (Easter: Sunday), April 8, A.D. 30.

The Ascension of Jesus, Thursday, May 18, A.D. 30.

Feast of Our Lady of Mt. Carmel
July 16, 1994
Rev. Albert Joseph Mary Shamon

Beginnings

BIRTH OF ST. JOSEPH

Through all time since Adam and no less in the years 35-25 B.C., sexual passion played a major role in history: Anthony had an adulterous affair with Cleopatra of Egypt and Herod the Great was madly in love with Mariamne, even though he had murdered her grandfather Hyrcanus and her brother Aristobolus.

Herod's sister, Salome, concocted a story about Mariamne being unfaithful, so Herod murdered her, too, and went almost mad with grief.

It was probably within the context of these sexual evils that the ever-chaste St. Joseph, head of the Holy Family, was born in Bethlehem of Judea between the years 35-25 B.C.

Joseph and Mary were betrothed about 7 B.C.

Joseph was probably 25 years old at the time; Mary, about 14 or 15.

JOACHIM AND ANNE

The names of the parents of the Blessed Virgin Mary do not appear in the New Testament; but they do appear in one of the most reliable of the Apocrypha, *The Protoevangelium of James,* written not too long after the Gospel of St. John; that is, about A.D. 130-140.

Apocryphal books are those that falsely claim divine authorship.[1] *The Protoevangelium* is purported to be written

---

1. In Catholic usage, Apocrypha are books which have some resemblance to the canonical books in subject matter, but which had not been recognized as canonical by the Church.

by James, the Bishop of Jerusalem. Still, this writing on the infancy of Jesus was of great influence and very popular in the early Church. In it the names of Mary's parents are given as Joachim and Anne.

In view of the tenacious genealogical memory of ancient and rural peoples, and especially of the Jews, it is highly unlikely that the names of Mary's parents, Joachim and Anne, were forgotten or confused at this early date.

BIRTH OF MARY

Herod the Great began rebuilding the temple in Jerusalem in January, 19 B.C. The construction went on until A.D. 64.

Probably only a year or two before this rebuilding, the Blessed Virgin Mary was born in the little village of Nazareth about 21 or 20 B.C.

Herod was rebuilding a marble temple to the God of the Jews; whereas God Himself was building a *dignum habitaculum,* a fitting temple, to the Son of God by having Mary become immaculately conceived in the womb of good St. Anne.

As Herod's temple of stone and wood and costly ornaments was rising, she whose womb was to temple God incarnate was growing at the same time.

THE ANNUNCIATION

God wanted His Son to enter the world like all other children, namely, by being born into a family. So He inspired the Virgin Mary to marry Joseph.

God also respects the free will of His children; so He sent the Angel Gabriel to win Mary's consent to becoming the mother of His Son.

The Angel Gabriel said, *"Hail, full of grace, the Lord is with you"* (*Lk.* 1:28).

The Greek *kecharitomene* means "one endowed with

favor or grace *(charis)* in a permanent way." So in the Revised Edition of the New Testament, instead of "Hail, full of grace," we have "Hail, favored one! The Lord is with you."

This translation indicates that a favor is meant here, far more than an ordinary one. Gabriel no doubt knew that Mary had been conceived immaculate in the womb of her mother the good St. Anne; and so He addressed her as highly favored. But he knew her to be doubly favored, because his mission was to ask her if she would become the Mother of the Son of God.

No doubt inspired by God, Mary had made a vow of perpetual virginity, for she questioned the angel, *"How can this be, since I have no relations with a man?"* The tense she used was the Aramaic active participle, which indicated she never intended to have relations with a man. Her words expressed not just a fact, but a determination never to use the privileges of married life. In fact, she was ready to forgo the inestimable honor of being the mother of God's Son if it meant the sacrifice of her virginity, even in the lawful use of marriage.

The angel understood her question that way, for he revealed to her that God's plan was that she be a virgin-mother, for her Son-to-be already had a Father in Heaven. Her child would be miraculously conceived, for the angel said: *"The Holy Spirit will come upon you, and the power of the Most High will overshadow you. Therefore the child to be born will be called holy, the Son of God."* Thus St. Ambrose said: "The first Adam came from the virgin earth; the second, from the virgin."

If Mary did not intend to have relations with a man, why did she marry St. Joseph?

First of all, she was submitting to the custom of her

nation. The Jews had a saying that "A girl should have one of two processions: either a wedding procession or a funeral procession." Mary yielded to custom, but she did not yield the principle: she married a man who had also vowed his virginity to God, St. Joseph.

Such a vow was not uncommon: the Essenes practiced it. The Essenes were a Jewish sect, living on the western shore of the Dead Sea, at the time of Jesus. They abstained from marriage. The historian Flavius Josephus said they were one of the three sects of the Jews; the other two were the Pharisees and the Sadducees.

Secondly, marriage was necessary for Mary lest she suffer the fate of an unwed mother. Then, too, she and her Child needed a provider and protector. Furthermore, Mary herself needed a companion, a comforter, a confidant, one with whom she could share the thoughts of her heart.

Mary could have said "No" to God's request through the angel. Lucifer said No! So did our first parents! And their No's have brought countless ills upon all mankind. Imagine what further calamities might have visited us had Mary also said No! We owe her an unpayable debt.

In her great love for God and for us, she said, "Yes!" By so doing she brought the Son of God to earth, and our redemption began in earnest. So great and joyful was this event that three times a day church bells ring and God's children pray the Angelus in joyful thanksgiving.

THE BIRTH OF JESUS

St. Matthew says that Jesus was born *"in the days of King Herod" (Mt. 2:1)*. We know for certain that Herod died in Jericho a few days before the Passover of March/April, 4 B.C.

The coming of the Magi, the massacre of the babies of Bethlehem, and the flight of the Holy Family into Egypt—

all occurred prior to the death of Herod, while he was still in Jerusalem. The order to slay all the boys in Bethlehem and its vicinity, two years old and under, was based on the time that Herod had carefully ascertained from the Magi.

Even granting that Herod as a precaution had extended the age to be certain to include his victim, the infant Jesus must have been at least one year old, if not more, when these events occurred.

Apparently, Herod was in good health when the Magi came to him in Jerusalem, for he bade the Magi bring back word about the birth of the newborn king so that he, too, could go and do him homage. This had to be earlier than six months before his death, because six months before his death, the king was gravely ill and was taken to Jericho to seek a cure at the hot springs there.

This information implies that Jesus was eighteen months old at the time of Herod's death. Hence Jesus was born, at the latest, in September, 6 B.C.

Two other pieces of information confirm this assumption. First, the astronomical evidence regarding the star of Bethlehem. Data from astronomy show us that in 6 B.C., Jupiter, Saturn, and Mars were in conjunction in the con-stellation Pisces. They would have appeared to the naked eye as a very bright star. This phenomenon occurs only once every 800 years.

Secondly, the **census** at Jesus' birth. *"This was the first enrollment when Quirinius was governor of Syria"* (*Lk.* 2:2). Quirinius was governor of Syria twice: once before 8 B.C. and once after A.D. 4. Saturninus was governor of Syria from 8 to 6 B.C. Now Quirinius could have begun the census in 9 B.C., which Saturninus could have completed in 6 B.C. Or Saturninus could have begun the census in 6 B.C. completed by Quirinius in 3 B.C.

Tertullian says the census was under Saturninus. This

could well have been. But Roman governors often were assisted by one who was second in command for specific purposes, like a census. Under Saturninus, Quirinius was second in command, for he was the military commander in the region. He could have been the one executing the census.

Most likely, Jesus was not born before 6 B.C. because St. Luke says, *"When Jesus began his ministry he was about 30 years of age"* (3:23). Dating Jesus' birth at 6 B.C. makes Him about 33 years old at the beginning of His public ministry in A.D. 28.

DEATH OF ST. JOSEPH

Tradition has it that St. Joseph died in A.D. 15. Jesus was about 20 years old then. So for more than a decade, Jesus supported His mother by his carpentering.

Note

DATE OF JESUS' BIRTH

Jesus was born during the reign of the Roman Emperor Augustus (31 B.C.-A.D. 14). Herod the Great had been appointed king by the Romans and ruled in Jerusalem from 40 to 4 B.C.

The visit of the Magi (*Mt.* 2:1) and Herod's slaughter of the innocents (*Mt.* 2:16) place the birth of Christ about two years before Herod's death in 4 B.C., which would be about 7 or 6 B.C. This date is contrary to the present calendar which had a serious error in calculation.

Dionysius Exiguus (A.D. 500-550), a Scythian monk, erroneously placed the year of Jesus' birth in 754 a.u.c. These letters are an abbreviation for *ad urbe condita* ("from the founding of the city" of Rome). It is now a fact that Herod had died four years earlier, in 750 a.u.c., and so Jesus was not born in 754 a.u.c. or the year one.

The day and month of Jesus' birth was put on December 25 in A.D. 325 to replace the boisterous pagan feast of *Sol invictus* ("The Unconquered Sun"), which was celebrated at the time of the winter solstice (after December 22).

But since Jesus was born during the taking of a census, the month of September or October would actually have been a more accurate choice. At that time, the harvesting would be finished and the winter rains would not yet have made the roads and valleys impassable.

PART I

THE FOUNDING OF
THE KINGDOM—
THE CHURCH

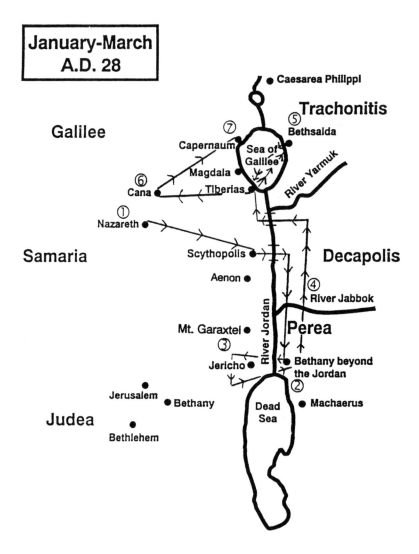

January-March A.D. 28

Caesarea Philippi

Trachonitis

Galilee

⑤ Bethsaida

Capernaum ⑦

Sea of Galilee

Magdala

River Yarmuk

⑥ Cana

Tiberias

① Nazareth

Samaria

Scythopolis

Decapolis

Aenon

④ River Jabbok

River Jordan

Mt. Garaxtel

Perea

③

Jericho

Bethany beyond the Jordan

② Machaerus

Jerusalem ● Bethany

Dead Sea

Judea

Bethlehem

Parables in November followed by miracles in December.

① Jesus leaves Nazareth for Bethany beyond the Jordan
② Baptism of Jesus
③ Temptations of Jesus
④ Jesus calls first disciples
⑤ Bethsaida
⑥ Wedding at Cana
⑦ At Capernaum to go to Jerusalem for Passover

2

Chapter 1

The Beginning of the Public Ministry of Jesus

Jesus had two objectives in mind for His earthly life. The first was to redeem the world by His passion, death, and resurrection. This objective John pointed out by referring to Him as "the Lamb of God, who takes away the sin of the world."

His second objective was to found a kingdom (His Church), in order that His redemption might be brought to all peoples of all times and all places.

As noted earlier, Jesus began with His second objective first. He laid the foundation of this kingdom by calling to Himself some of John's disciples and by confirming their faith in Him by the miracle at Cana. The Latin word for Church is *ecclesia,* which simply means "to call," "to gather people" to oneself.

JOHN PREPARES THE WAY FOR JESUS

The word of God came to John in the desert in the fifteenth year of the reign of Tiberius Caesar (*Lk.* 3:1). Augustus Caesar died August 19, A.D. 14, and Tiberius succeeded him. In Syria the new year began in October. Since August to October would be considered the first year of Tiberius' reign, the fifteenth year of Tiberius Caesar would be October, A.D. 27. (See NOTE at end of chapter.)

John baptized on the western bank of the Jordan river, four and one half miles north of the Dead Sea (*Lk.* 3:15-22). Fearless, like Elijah, he called a spade a spade. He branded the Pharisees and Sadducees a "brood of vipers" (*Mt.* 3:7). He instructed the crowds, the tax collectors, the soldiers as

3

to what they must do to be saved (*Lk.* 3:10-14). And with the humility of a prophet, he declared again and again he was not the Messiah—only His voice, one not worthy to carry His sandals (*Mt.* 3:11-12).

JESUS IS BAPTIZED AND TEMPTED

Word of John's preaching reached Galilee. So, probably in the month of December, a crowd left Galilee to go to hear the voice crying in the wilderness. Jesus was with the crowd. The pilgrim group probably traveled to Scythopolis, crossed the Jordan, and proceeded along the east bank to Bethany beyond the Jordan where John was baptizing. Jesus was lost among the pilgrims; even John did not recognize Him, until he had received a revelation when he baptized Jesus around January or February A.D. 28.

Jesus willed to be baptized by John in order to identify Himself with all sinners; and also in order to prepare His followers for His baptism of water and the Spirit, which would open the heavens to the baptized and makes them beloved sons of God.

After His baptism, *"Jesus was led by the Spirit into the desert to be tempted by the devil"* (*Mt.* 4:10-11). Tradition indicates that the place of the first and third temptations of Jesus was the Mount of Qarantal, rising behind old Jericho.

The temptations were related to His baptism. At His baptism, the voice from Heaven said, "This is my beloved Son." Satan, you can be sure, had been there snooping around. So twice in tempting Jesus, Satan asked, "If you are the Son of God . . ." He was trying to find out. He doesn't know everything.

The temptations of Jesus were a terrible solicitation to the sin of pride. In Eden man wanted to be like God, so God became like man. God emptied Himself and took the form of a slave. What the devil was doing was asking Jesus to throw off the limitations of a man; and, if He were the Son of God, to act like God by working all kinds of miracles. The devil was saying in effect, "If you are the Son of God, show it. Break the bonds of your humanity. Act like God and not like man. Do not accept the restrictions of your human nature. Take the easy way out."

The astuteness of the demon! He knew if Jesus did this, He would have fallen like the first Adam. But even more subtly, he knew if Jesus did this, people would be following Him, not out of love, but out of curiosity.

It is interesting to note that the devil was willing to give the whole world for a single soul.The summit of the Mount of Qarantal offers a magnificent view of the Jordan valley and the land of Moab. Here the devil showed Jesus all the kingdoms of the world and said, *"All these I shall give to you, if you will prostrate yourself and worship me"* (*Mt.* 4:8-9). Dr. Faustus in Marlowe's play succumbed to this temptation, as have so many after him. Jesus conquered the tempter by prayer, fasting, and the words of Sacred Scripture.

JOHN PROCLAIMS THE MISSION OF JESUS

After His victory, Jesus came down from the mountain of temptation and went back to Bethany beyond the Jordan where John was still baptizing (*Jn.* 1:28).

Before Jesus arrived there, the Jews from Jerusalem had sent priests and Levites to question John about his being the Messiah. John vehemently declared that he was not the Messiah. Yet, putting great stock on externals, many of the Jewish religious leaders ignored John's denials. After all, John was of noble descent, son of a high priest. Then too, his way of life was austere: he was dressed in camel skin with a leather girdle around his waist, he fed on locusts and wild honey, condemned material things, and spoke with the fire and zeal of a prophet. So judging by externals, he had what they believed to be all the earmarks of a prophet.

So the Jewish religious leaders persisted. They sent to him their most honored ones, the Jerusalem priests and Levites, hoping to sway him into proclaiming that he was the Christ.

John was not seduced. With great humility, he thundered, *"I am not the Christ! I'm only the voice of one crying in the wilderness. I'm not the Word, only the echo"* (*John* 1:19-28).

The next day when Jesus walked by, John testified to the crowds and the Jerusalem delegates, *"Behold the Lamb of God, who takes away the sin of the world. He, not I, is the one who is the Son of God"* (*Jn.* 1:29-34). With that forthright declaration, John rested his case.

THE FIRST DISCIPLES OF JESUS

On the day following John's clear announcement about the Lamb of God, Jesus walked by. As He did, the Baptist said to two of his disciples, Andrew and John, "Behold the Lamb of God!" The two disciples heard him speak, and they followed Jesus. Jesus sensed He was being followed, so He turned and said to them, "What are you looking for?" They answered, "Rabbi, where do you live?" Jesus invited them to come and see. It was about four in the afternoon. They stayed with Him that day.

Jesus convinced them that they had found the Messiah, so Andrew went to fetch his brother Simon. When Jesus saw Simon, He said, *"You are Simon the son of John. You will be called Cephas"* (which is translated Peter) (*John* 1:42). St. John wrote that Andrew *"first* found his own brother Simon . . ."* The implication was that immediately after, both Andrew and John found John's own brother James. Eventually these four would grow into the twelve— the foundation stones of His Church.

The next day, Jesus and His four disciples went to Galilee. Jesus wanted to see His mother; the four were eager to return to their own homes in Bethsaida to tell their dear ones all that had transpired in the past few weeks.

Very possibly the little group went to Tiberias where the disciples had moored their boat. They then sailed to Bethsaida, northeast of the Lake of Tiberias (also known as the Sea of Galilee), near where the Jordan enters the Lake.

At Bethsaida, these four proclaimed the news that they had found the Messiah. The news spread like wildfire around the village. All wanted to see Jesus. One lad came whose name was Philip. When Jesus saw him, He said to him, "Follow me"; and Jesus meant this to be for always. Philip did.

Fired also with enthusiasm, Philip found his friend Nathaniel. To him Philip burst out, "We've found the One about whom Moses and the prophets spoke, Jesus of Nazareth." Nathaniel was from Cana, and rivalry existed between Cana and Nazareth, so Nathaniel smirked, "Can anything good come out of Nazareth?" Nathaniel knew his Scriptures and Scripture said that the Messiah would come out of Bethlehem. The guileless Philip didn't argue; he merely said, "Come and see." Nathaniel came, so great was his desire to leave no stone unturned. He came and saw and was conquered (*Jn.* 1:43-51).

Note how all these first disciples had been seeking the Messiah. Our Lord said, "Seek and you shall find." And that is exactly what happened to Andrew and Philip: they were searching and they found. *"We have found . . ."* (*Jn.* 1:41,45). *"Blessed are those who hunger and thirst for holiness; they'll find it."*

Also, one of the most effective ways to evangelize is person to person—the apostolate of one on one, of like on like. It's the old idea: make a friend, be a friend, and bring that friend to Christ.

John the Baptist brought Andrew and John to Christ.

Andrew brought Peter. Andrew and John brought James. These four touched Philip. Philip brought his friend Nathaniel. It's the gospel way of evangelizing: friend on friend.

Nathaniel, the friend of Philip, was probably the apostle Bartholomew. Only John in his Gospel mentions Nathaniel, the other Gospels do not. But they list Bartholomew among the apostles, whereas John never mentions him. In the listing of the apostles in the synoptic Gospels, Bartholomew is usually named with Philip, the friend of Nathaniel. It is very probable that Bartholomew is a surname for Nathaniel meaning the son of Tholmai.

THE WEDDING AT CANA, MARCH, A.D. 28

On the third day after meeting Nathaniel, Jesus went to Cana for a wedding. Possibly, He went by boat from Bethsaida to Tiberias; then walked the two or three hours to Cana.

At Cana, six miles northwest of Nazareth, Jesus joined His mother there at the wedding feast held in the home of the groom. Like a good mother and housewife, Mary was probably helping with serving the food when she noticed the wine was running short. That would have been catastrophic and a great disgrace for the wedding couple. The festivities would have ended abruptly, like the lights going out at the climax of a play.

Mary saw the situation and foresaw how terrible the embarrassment would be for the young couple. So she hurried to Jesus and said simply, "They have no wine"—as if amazed that her Son had done nothing about it.

Jesus answered, "Woman, how does your concern affect me? My hour has not yet come."

He addressed her as "woman" to identify her with the woman in *Genesis* who would crush the serpent's head.

And He said, "Why are you discussing this with me?"

The Greek reads, "What to me and to thee?" The sense depends largely on the tone of voice and the facial expression. Here it may mean, "No problem. I'm of the same mind and will. I'll see to it. All will be well." Then, as if to explain why He had not done anything so far, He went on to say, "Did you not know that my hour had not yet come, that it was to come only after you had asked me?" Jesus seemed to imply that His miracles would not begin until Mary had intervened—to show that blessings in the future were to come through her intercession.

Thus the first miracle of grace—the sanctification of John the Baptist in the womb of his mother Elizabeth—began with Mary. Likewise, God willed that the first miracle of nature also begin with her here at Cana.

Mary understood Jesus' reply that way, so she said to the servers, "Do whatever he tells you." They did; they filled six waterpots with water, each waterpot holding from twenty to thirty gallons. Jesus changed the water into wine, and *"his disciples began to believe in him"* (*Jn.* 2:11).

Commenting on this miracle, Fyodor Dostoyevsky said that the first miracle of Jesus was not to heal the sick, nor raise the dead, but to save a young couple from embarrassment, because He wanted to teach us about the sanctity of marriage and bring domestic joy to the world.

Another of the lessons of Cana was to teach us the power of Mary's intercession. The Church has already defined four dogmas about Mary: the Council of Ephesus (431) declared Mary is the *Mother of God;* the Lateran Council (647) defined that she is *Ever-Virgin;* Pius IX (1854) defined the dogma of her *Immaculate Conception;* and Pius XII (1950) defined her *Assumption.* A further dogma regarding Mary, currently under study, is the *Mediatrix of all graces.* It would probably state that since she is the "Gate of Heaven," all that comes from Heaven to earth passes through her; all that goes from earth to Heaven passes through her.

For us the lesson of Cana is that, like the servants, we must always bring the water of our efforts to seek spiritual growth. Only after we have done our best, filled the jars to the brim, will God step in and crown our efforts with the joy of discipleship.

In the Catholic celebration of the Holy Eucharist, a few drops of water are changed into wine at the Presentation of the Gifts. Then the host and the wine are changed into the Body and Blood of Christ at the Consecration. Finally, at Holy Communion the bread and wine are received to give a joy, not unlike that of guests at a wedding feast. *"Wine gladdens men's hearts"* (*Ps.* 104:15).

Marriage was the symbol of God's covenant with His people in the Old Testament. It, too, is the symbol of Christ's covenant with His Church in the New Testament. But as wine surpasses water, so does the New Testament surpass the Old, for Christ's union with His Church is renewed sacramentally each day when bread and wine are changed into His body and blood.

After the wedding feast, Jesus, His mother, His brethren (His cousins), and His disciples went to Capernaum about 20 miles from Cana (*Jn.* 2:12). Capernaum was a natural rendezvous for pilgrims forming into caravans for the paschal journey to Jerusalem. Jesus stayed there a few days to provide for the care of His mother. Then He headed for Jerusalem in one of the caravans in order to begin His public life at the Passover of March A.D. 28.

Note

Tiberius had exiled himself to Capri in A.D. 26 and appointed Pontius Pilate governor of Judea A.D. 26-36.

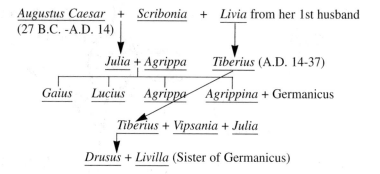

Augustus Caesar + *Scribonia* + *Livia* from her 1st husband
(27 B.C. -A.D. 14)

Julia + *Agrippa*   *Tiberius* (A.D. 14-37)

Gaius   *Lucius*   *Agrippa*   *Agrippina* + Germanicus

Tiberius + *Vipsania* + *Julia*

Drusus + *Livilla* (Sister of Germanicus)

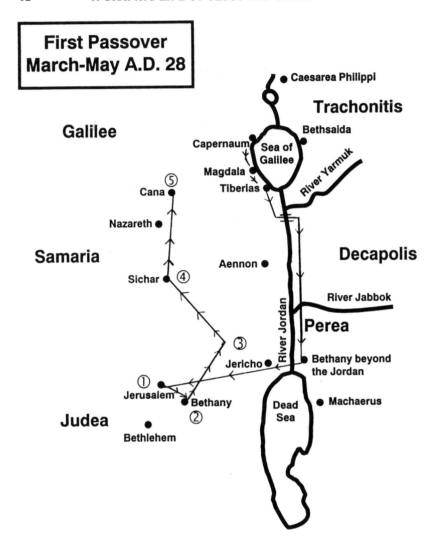

**First Passover
March-May A.D. 28**

① Cleanses the Temple
② Nicodemus
③ Judean Ministry
④ Samaritan Woman
⑤ Second miracle at Cana

Chapter 2

Hints Regarding the Nature of His Kingdom

EARLY MINISTRY IN JUDEA

There were three Passovers in the life of Jesus: (1) at the beginning of His public life A.D. 28; (2) at the middle of His public life A.D. 29; and (3) at the end, A.D. 30. The first Passover began Tuesday, March 30, A.D. 28.

As St. Paul went to the synagogues first, then to the Gentiles, so Jesus went to the center of religion for God's chosen people—Jerusalem. He would give His own every chance to be His Church. But He found that their interpretation of God's religion was rotten to the core. Later, in His Sermon of the Mount, He would say to His disciples that unless their justice surpassed that of the scribes and Pharisees they would not enter the kingdom of Heaven. Thus, one of His very first public acts was to clean house in God's temple.

JESUS CLEANSES THE TEMPLE

On the occasion of a great feast, like that of Passover, the Court of the Gentiles in the Temple became a veritable stockyard, a noisy, smelly marketplace. Not only were sacrificial animals, bellowing oxen, bleating lambs, and cooing doves, being sold there; but financial transactions were also going on—Greek and Roman coins had to be exchanged for Tyrian coins, the only kind acceptable for paying the annual Temple Tax.

Every Jew over nineteen had to pay the Temple Tax. This tax was necessary to defray the expenses for the daily temple sacrifices. The tax was one half-shekel, two days' wages; but it had to be paid in temple currency.

Now, during the Passover, Jewish pilgrims came from all over the ancient world. Their coins with imperial and pagan images on them were considered unclean for the Temple Tax. Money changers in the temple would exchange these coins for acceptable ones. But these money changers were often swindlers, no better than thieves, charging exorbitant rates of exchange. Thus Jesus lashed out at them and said, "My house shall be a house of prayer, but you are making it a den of thieves."

The priests did nothing at all about this noisy traffic in the sacred precincts because it meant money to them.

But Jesus, however, at the sights and the sounds that smothered the hymns and prayers going on in the Inner Court, could not contain Himself. Zeal for His Father's house consumed Him. In a burst of righteous anger, He cleaned house. He was angry not so much at the people engaged in buying and selling as with what had happened to religion—it had been reduced to offering animal sacrifices, leaving the heart so untouched, that even dishonesty was countenanced.

Jesus just couldn't stand by. When He had expelled the traffickers, the Jews asked, "What sign can you show us for doing this?" Jesus answered, *"Destroy this temple."* (It was as if He said, "Get rid of this Old Testament religion that you have built, in which God is worshiped by offering things and not oneself, and in which stealing is sanctioned. Destroy it!")

Then Jesus went on, *". . . in three days I will raise it up."* He implied, "I will establish a new covenant, a new order in which the center of religion will not be a temple, a stone building, consisting of offering things to God, but a Person, I, Jesus Christ, the Son of God, with love at the heart of it."

Blinded with pride, the enemies of Jesus took Him literally and retorted, *"This temple has been under construction 46 years, and you will raise it up in three days?"* (*John* 2:18-20).

This remark helps us to date Our Lord's ministry. Herod began rebuilding the temple around 20-19 B.C. Therefore, 46 years later, the first Passover in Jesus' public ministry would be that of March 30, A.D. 28.

(Matthew, Mark, and Luke place the cleansing of the temple in Holy Week because in their Gospel that was the first time Jesus came to Jerusalem. John's placing it here is probably the correct spot, see pp. 122-124).

JESUS TALKS WITH NICODEMUS, BETHANY, APRIL, A.D. 28

At this time many God-fearing Jews lived in Jerusalem. The defilement of the temple disturbed them too. But they did nothing—either they lacked the courage or feared the retaliatory power of the Sanhedrin. How elated they were when they saw this tall Galilean, strong from years of carpentering, majestic in bearing, fearlessly fulminating against them like one of the prophets of old! One of them, Nicodemus, even came to Him afterwards at night.

During His visits to Jerusalem, Jesus made the home of Lazarus, at Bethany, his headquarters. Lazarus was wealthy, and the brother of Mary and Martha; and these three were among the dearest friends of Jesus. They opened their home to Him and His disciples. It was to Lazarus' home that Nicodemus came to Jesus at night. At night, perhaps out of fear of the religious establishment of which he was a member, or more likely because he could get to speak with Jesus alone only in the evening hour.

Nicodemus was very respectful: he called Jesus "Rabbi." He said, "We know . . ." and so represented a group who believed that Jesus was from God. Jesus, however, perceived the question that was on his mind and talked of how one might enter the Kingdom of God.

Jesus said to him, "Amen, amen, I say to you, no one can see the kingdom of God without being born from above." The Greek adverb *anothen* can mean "again" or "from above." Both meanings are true and both are intended.

Nicodemus took Jesus literally; he thought Jesus was speaking of a physical rebirth. Jesus explained that He was talking of a spiritual rebirth, of water and the Holy Spirit. He went on to say that like begets like: flesh begets flesh and spirit begets spirit.

When a husband sows the seeds of life in the good earth of his wife's womb, and God creates a soul, then a child is conceived—"flesh begets flesh."

When God the Father sows the seed of the Holy Spirit in a child's soul when it is baptized, the Spirit, through sanctifying grace, transforms that soul so that it becomes truly a child of God—Spirit begets spirit.

Perhaps as Jesus and Nicodemus were speaking, an evening breeze blew. Great teacher that He was, Jesus used this refreshing breeze to explain that the Spirit and His activities are like the wind: you can't see the wind, but you can feel its effects; you can't control the wind, it comes and goes as it will. So the Spirit is unseen, but His works are not; and He is free—He comes and goes as He wills and to whom He wills.

Nicodemus was puzzled, but deeply impressed by the wisdom and holiness of Jesus. Later, he defended Jesus before the Sanhedrin (*Jn.* 7:50-51); then after the crucifixion of Jesus, he threw all caution to the winds and dared to assist Joseph of Arimathea in burying Him.

JESUS' MINISTRY OUTSIDE JERUSALEM, APRIL-MAY, A.D. 28

Nicodemus' visit was like a shot in the arm for Jesus, so

He decided to remain in the area of Judea for a time. Because of the enmity of the leaders in Jerusalem, Jesus retreated somewhat to the north of the city, to the Jordan valley near Jericho, where there was much water. He remained there for the month of April. His disciples were baptizing like John. Many people joined Him, some from the ranks of John the Baptist.

John the Baptist was baptizing around Aenon in the upper Jordan valley, about eight miles south of Scythopolis. Aenon means "springs," for there were many springs there. Near Rochester, New York, we call a small village with healing waters "Clifton Springs."

When the Baptist's disciples saw Jesus gaining in popularity, they grew sad and said to John, "Rabbi, the one who was with you across the Jordan is baptizing and everyone is coming to him." John reminded them again, "I am not the Messiah! I'm the best man for the bridegroom. He must increase; I must decrease. To see this happening is my joy." No wonder Jesus said of John, *". . . among those born of women, no one is greater than John"* (*Lk.* 7:28).

As a matter of fact, John did decrease by being decapitated; and Jesus did increase by being lifted up on the cross.

The zealous and fiery John the Baptist spared no one in his rebukes, not even Herod Antipas. In consequence, John was arrested in May, A.D. 28 and imprisoned in the mighty fortress of Macherus, east of the Dead Sea, in Perea, the territory of Herod. This served as a signal for Jesus to launch His ministry in full earnest. He picked Galilee to be the scene of His ministry for the next 18 months. Jesus returned to Galilee by taking the road that ran through the center of Palestine across Samaria. He took this route to avoid Herod.

JESUS AND THE SAMARITAN WOMAN (Jn. 4:1-42)

On His way through Samaria, Jesus encountered a Samaritan woman at Sychar, at the well of Jacob.

Samaritans were despised by Jews because they were considered racially impure and theologically heretical.

But Jesus was a people's person. He put people before anything else, even rules and regulations. Jews weren't supposed to talk to Samaritans, but Jesus did! Rabbis weren't supposed to talk to women in public, but Jesus did! He went even further—He asked a Samaritan woman for a drink. Even she wondered, "You, a Jew, ask me, a Samaritan?"

Jesus thirsted for her soul and offered her living water, more than she could give Him. To her, living water meant fresh, running water as against stagnant water. Jesus meant the Holy Spirit, given to those washed clean in the waters of baptism.

Her wayward life prevented her from receiving this living water. So Jesus told her to call her husband in order to put her moral life in order. She no doubt did, for Jesus led her gradually to see who He was: first she called Him "Jew," then "Sir," then "Prophet," then "Messiah."

Having been evangelized by Him, she in turn became an evangelist and brought her village to Him as "the Savior of the world."

Jesus stayed with the Samaritans two days, but worked no miracles there to convert them, for His mission was to the house of Israel. Furthermore, this was not yet the appropriate time: He was still laying the foundation of His Church, and the apostles had not yet been sufficiently trained to teach all nations. So Jesus bided His time. He knew that later, when the Spirit would come upon His Church, the apostles would send Philip to evangelize the Samaritans (*Acts* 8:5-8).

So Jesus left the Samaritans, well disposed toward Himself, and journeyed to Cana of Galilee about 20 miles northeast of Sychar, a seven hour trip by foot.

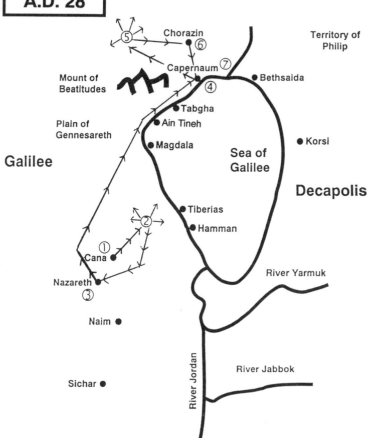

① In Cana Jesus cures an official's boy
② Galilean ministry (south) He began to preach
    in the synagogues of Galilee
③ Nazareth: first visit
④ Capernaum—miracles: fish
                demoniac
                Peter's mother-in-law
⑤ Galilean ministry (north) *Let us go to the nearby towns*
    that I may preach there also
⑥ Jesus cures a leper.
⑦ Five conflicts with the Scribes and Pharisees

Chapter 3

Launching the Kingdom in Galilee
(Early Galilean Ministry)

THE SECOND MIRACLE AT CANA, MAY, A.D. 28

As Jesus journeyed to Cana, He was greeted enthusiastically all along the way. It had been a month since He had driven the money-changers out of the temple in Jerusalem at the paschal feast. His fearlessness, His dignity, His bearing, His grace, His zeal—all these had made a profound impact on His fellow Galileans. When He arrived in Galilee everyone was still talking of how He had bearded the lions in their own den. They were proud of Him!

Jesus did not stop at Nazareth but went directly on to Cana because Mary apparently was still there. At Cana a royal official of Herod Antipas, Chusa, the husband of Joanna (*Lk.* 8:13), came to Jesus beseeching Him to come down to Capernaum to heal his little boy who was on the point of death. Cana was about 870 feet above sea level, whereas Capernaum was 680 feet below sea level.

The royal official's faith was weak. He seemed to think that Jesus had to go down in person to Capernaum to heal his little boy. Then, too, he pleaded so urgently, as if every minute counted—"Come before my little boy dies"—as though Jesus had no power over death. But weak faith or not, he came to Jesus—any port in a storm.

Jesus saw that the official's faith was weak; he was demanding His presence, as if He could not act from a distance. But ever sensitive to people's failings and feelings,

Jesus did not embarrass him by calling attention to his weakness. Instead, in a gentle, matter-of-fact way He gave the official a chance to make an act of faith by having him take His word. For Jesus simply said, "Go, your little boy lives." The official believed, and the little boy was cured because of his father's faith. The miracle caused the official and his whole household to believe in Jesus.

How often the sickness of a loved one has brought a family to Christ!

JESUS PREACHES IN THE SYNAGOGUES OF GALILEE

After this second miracle at Cana, Jesus began to preach in the south and west of Galilee. In the synagogues there, He said, *"Repent and believe in the gospel"* (*Mk.* 1:15). John began his preaching by the banks of the Jordan; Jesus began His preaching in the synagogues of Galilee. John preached repentance; Jesus preached repentance and faith.

At this time, Jesus made His first visit to Nazareth. He was well received this time. *"All spoke highly of him and were amazed at the gracious words that came from his mouth"* (*Lk.* 4:22). When He went back to Nazareth seven months later, the reception was totally different: they tried to kill Him (*Lk.* 4:28).

After this first visit, Jesus left Nazareth for Capernaum. He *"went to live in Capernaum by the sea in the region of Zebulum and Naphtali"* (*Mt.* 4:13).

One thing Jesus learned in carpentering was to plan. He knew He needed a base of operations to launch the kingdom. In Jerusalem, He chose Bethany for His headquarters; in Galilee, He chose Capernaum. The secluded town of Nazareth was fitting for His hidden life, but the cosmopolitan city of Capernaum served better for His public ministry. Through Capernaum ran the roads leading from Damascus to Egypt; it had a custom house and a Roman garrison.

In fact, a God-fearing Roman centurion had built the synagogue in Capernaum. In that synagogue, Jesus preached; and *"the crowds were astonished at his teaching, for he taught them as one having authority, and not as their scribes"* (*Mt.* 7:28-29).

THE MIRACULOUS CATCH OF FISH, MAY, A.D. 28

When not in the synagogue, Jesus walked along the shore of the lake, south of Capernaum. Crowds mobbed Him. To get some breathing room, He got into Peter's boat and used it as a pulpit. When He had finished teaching the crowds, He said to Simon, *"Put out into deep water and lower your nets for a catch"* (*Lk.* 5:4).

Peter replied, "Master, we have fished all night and caught nothing. But if you say so, we'll do it." When they did, they caught so many fish that their nets were tearing.

Peter then realized the great sanctity of Jesus and declared his own unworthiness, calling Him "Lord" now instead of "Master." "Depart from me, Lord, for I am a sinful man."

Using a pun, Jesus said, "You are fishermen; I will make you fishers of men." So Peter, Andrew, James and John left all and followed Him.

Peter had fished at night, the right time for fishing; Jesus fished at day, the wrong time for fishing. Peter had no success, yet Jesus had marvelous success.

Jesus was training his future fishers of men. The miracle eloquently said to them that, as in the catching of fish, so in the capturing of men, God's ways will often be found to be at variance with human standards. Still, His ways will always be best. All they need do is to have absolute trust in God and surrender to His will.

THE DEMONIAC AND PETER'S MOTHER-IN-LAW MAY, A.D. 28

Within a month or so, Jesus would call the twelve apostles

to Himself. And He would tell them that they are to cast out devils and cure sicknesses. But like any great teacher, Jesus demonstrated how to do this. So much of what He was saying and doing now was for the benefit of these pupils of His who were to carry on His work.

Thus in the synagogue of Capernaum, He cast out devils. The powers of darkness felt Jesus was a threat to their kingdom, they felt His holiness, they sensed the power emanating from His goodness. They were alarmed; so they marshalled all their forces against Him. In the synagogue no less, an unclean demon shrieked out at Him, crying out in a loud voice, *"What have you to do with us, Jesus of Nazareth? Have you come to destroy us?"* The unclean demon spoke of "us," for he was not alone, there were many others with him.

Jesus, like a mighty monarch, ordered the demon to leave the man (*Lk.* 4:33-37). The people were amazed, for He did this so easily. He used no spells, no elaborate ritual, no incantations, simply a command, *"Be quiet! Come out of the man!"* The demon obeyed! It was stupendous! Yet how ironic! Unclean spirits obeyed Him! Often people do not!

Later on, these exorcisms would create no more amazement than His other miracles. For familiarity does breed contempt.

Jesus left the synagogue around noon and went with His disciples to the house of Peter, probably for dinner. Simon's mother-in-law was afflicted with a severe fever. They asked Him to help her. Already their faith in Him was blossoming. Jesus willingly assented. He stood over her and commanded the fever to leave her. Her cure was instantaneous and complete, for *"she got up immediately and waited on them"* (*Lk.* 4:38-39).

What a lesson the disciples have given us: we ought to talk to God about our friends in need, as they did about Peter's mother-in-law.

What a lesson Peter's mother-in-law has given us: we ought always to give thanks to God for His blessings, by performing good works for others—"she waited on them."

After the sun had set, ending the Sabbath rest, the whole town gathered at Peter's house, bringing with them the possessed and those afflicted with various diseases. Jesus did not cure them en masse. He was concerned about each one of them individually; so he laid hands on each of them one by one and cured them all.

Jesus, however, never lost sight of His mission. That was why He arose the next morning before dawn and went to a deserted place to pray. To go on healing bodily ills mightly tempted Jesus, His compassion was so great. He felt the ailments of others deeply and never hesitated to alleviate them. His disciples and the citizens of Capernaum added to the temptation by clamoring for Him to return to the city and carry on this bodily apostolate.

But the Father had not sent Him to be a social worker, but to be a savior, to save people from their sins. Then, too, curing bodily ills is not necessarily the path to happiness; nor does it always bring souls to God—it didn't bring Capernaum!

Strengthened by prayer, Jesus resisted this temptation to reduce the Gospel to a social ministry. His disciples pleaded, "Everyone is looking for you." But the truth was, Jesus was looking for everyone; so He firmly said, *"Let us go to the nearby villages that I may preach there also"* (*Mk.* 1:38).

Jesus so wanted His future fishers of men to learn that the primary focus of His Church must not be on bodily ills, but on salvation—curing the ills of the soul. So He left Capernaum and started a missionary tour in northern Galilee.

JESUS HEALS A LEPER, MAY, A.D. 28
(Lk. 5:12-16; Mk. 1:41-45)

In those first few weeks, Jesus probably did not venture far from Capernaum. Bethsaida, Chorazin, and Magdala were all close by. In one of these towns, perhaps near Chorazin (two miles northwest of Capernaum), a leper came to Him. Luke, the physician, with medical exactness stated that the man was "full of leprosy." Leprosy ranged all the way from mere skin diseases to the incurable disease that eats away extremities (the hands and the feet) and covers the body with running sores till the flesh rots away. Luke indicates that the man had this latter kind of leprosy.

This leper, however, seemed to sense Jesus was different from other men, for he approached Him—a thing forbidden. He believed in Him, for he adored Him and said, "Lord, if you will, you can make me clean."

Moved with pity, Jesus stretched out His hands and touched him—also a thing forbidden. He wanted His future fishers-of-men to see that physical diseases are not evil, only sin is. People recoil from the hideousness of leprosy; but Jesus wanted His future leaders to recoil only from sin—never from the sinner.

Upon touching him, Jesus said, "I do will it. Be made clean." The leprosy left him immediately. Again Jesus was teaching His disciples that God does not will man's harm, but only his good.

No doubt Jesus explained to His disciples that leprosy can be seen as a symbol of sin. Leprosy torments the leper; sin torments the sinner. Leprosy banishes the leper from the society of others; sin alienates a person from God and his fellowman. As only He, Jesus, could cure the leper, so only He, Jesus, can forgive sin. As the leper came to Jesus seeking a cure, so the only condition for the cure of sin is that one go to Jesus—"present yourself to the priest." Jesus reminded the healed leper to go to the priest, out of respect for law and authority (*Lv.* 14:1-32).

He Himself withdrew to deserted places to pray, as was His habit. He hoped His example might teach His disciples never to let pastoral activities crowd out prayer. After some days, He returned to Capernaum.

HOSTILITY: SCRIBES AND PHARISEES, JUNE, A.D. 28

Jerusalem had opposed Jesus at the First Passover (*Jn.* 2:18). Jesus' success in Galilee, the enthusiasm of the crowds and the gathering of disciples round Him, moved the Jewish leaders in Jerusalem to send delegates to observe and report on Him.

They came to Capernaum not to follow Him, but to incriminate Him. Nothing Jesus said or did could satisfy or placate them. Every good deed of His was twisted and given an evil connotation. Their hostility mounted, driving Jesus to turn to unlettered fishermen on whom to build His Church.

Mark records this growing antagonism toward Jesus in five conflict stories.

The First Conflict: The Forgiveness of Sin
(*Mk.* 2:1-12)

Four men brought a paralytic to Jesus. Because of their faith, Jesus said, "Child, your sins are forgiven."

The attitude of the scribes and Pharisees for Jesus was evident in their reference to Him as "this man"—a term of contempt (*Mk.* 2:7). They reasoned in their hearts that "this man blasphemes. Who can forgive sins but only God?"

With great humility, Jesus, who had read their hearts and had seen their unkind thoughts, tried to lead them to the truth, to show that He had the power to forgive sins. He did something that would have convinced any good-willed person: He worked a miracle they all could see, namely, He cured the paralytic, to prove He could work the miracle they could not see, namely that of forgiving sins.

If His enemies learned nothing from this, His disciples did, for on the first Easter Sunday eve they understood what

He had meant when He gave them the Holy Spirit and the power to forgive sins as well.

The Second Conflict:
He Chooses a Sinner for a Disciple

Levi was a tax collector. In the eyes of the Jews, all who helped the hated Romans to collect taxes were sinners. Jesus had forgiven sin, now He called a sinner to be His disciple.

Levi, or Matthew, lived in Tabgha, a mile or two south of Capernaum. In his home there, this "sinner" threw a dinner for Jesus, to which he invited his own friends, other tax collectors, also branded sinners by the Jews. Jesus accepted the invitation and ate with "sinners."

Typical of the cowardly Pharisees, they did not attack Jesus directly; rather, they sniped at Him behind His back, questioning His disciples, *"Why does your teacher eat with tax-collectors and sinners?"* The innuendo was that their Master was a sinner also. Jesus heard their snide remark and said, *"The well do not need a physician but the sick do."*

Then just as heresy often occasions the definition of dogma, so conflict caused Jesus to state clearly what His mission was, especially for the sake of His disciples, *"I did not come to call the righteous but sinners"* (*Mk.* 2:13-17).

The Third Conflict: Jesus Acts Like a Sinner—
He Doesn't Fast (*Mk.* 2:18-22)

Mosaic Law prescribed only one day of fasting a year— the Day of Atonement (*Lv.* 16:29). But the Pharisees fasted weekly, on Mondays and Thursdays. So the people came to Jesus, and, seeing Him and His disciples banqueting with Levi, objected, "Why do the disciples of John and those of the Pharisees fast while yours do not?"

In answering them, Jesus used the same image as John the Baptist, namely, that of a wedding. The Incarnation was a wedding of divine and human natures. A wedding, as anyone knows, is a time of joy and festivity. Fasting, a sign of sorrow and penance, is patently inappropriate.

Then for the benefit of His disciples, Jesus explained why He was founding a Church: it was impossible to try to wed the new with the old. That would be like patching an old garment with new cloth or pouring new wine into old wineskins. New cloth when washed would shrink and make a greater tear; new wine would ferment and burst old wineskins.

Jesus went on to teach, not only the people, but especially His disciples, that His Church would bring something brand new. This newness would require new men, open minds, and open hearts, untouched by traditional prejudices. This Church was to be animated by the Spirit—bringing a life totally different from the brand of religion taught by the Pharisees.

His church would call for a fasting, for instance, that was a sincere expression of repentance, not a showy display of righteousness. The religion of His Church, too, was to be not mere ritualism or externalism, but a matter of the heart, of love of God and neighbor, expressed by service.

The Fourth Conflict: He Breaks the Sabbath, June, A.D. 28 (*Mk.* 2:23-28)

A short walk of one half mile was permitted on the Sabbath. A month before, after His talk with the Samaritan woman, Jesus had said the fields were ripe for the harvest (*Jn.* 4:35). Walking through a ripe grain field, the disciples of Jesus plucked some grain, rubbed it in their hands to get rid of the chaff, then ate it. The Pharisees were furious. To them plucking grain and chaffing it was tantamount to harvesting and reaping—things forbidden on the Sabbath.

Jesus instantly came to the defense of His own. He pointed out that necessity knows no law. To illustrate, He cited how, when David and his soldiers were hungry, they ate the loaves of proposition reserved for the priests (*1 Sam.* 21:2-7). Then to nail down His argument, Jesus reminded them that the priests themselves worked on the Sabbath by offering sacrifice to the Lord (*Num.* 28:9). To sum up, He enunciated the principle: "The sabbath was made for man, not man for the sabbath."

The Fifth Conflict: He Breaks the Sabbath Again, June, A.D. 28 (*Mk.* 3:1-5)

Having been worsted at every turn by Jesus, the fury of the Pharisees knew no bounds. All they saw in their confrontation with Jesus was a power conflict, not an invitation to salvation. They would get Him one way or the other. Very likely they planted a man with a shriveled hand in the synagogue to see if Jesus would break the Sabbath by healing him. They knew His compassion.

There was no pressing need for a cure on this day. Yet Jesus cured the man that His disciples might learn how wrong were the principles of their enemies. For instance, He asked them, "Is it permitted to do a good deed on the Sabbath—or an evil one? To preserve a life—or to destroy it?" In other words, must good be avoided to keep the letter of the law or must evil be done by refraining from a good action just to keep the letter of the law?

They remained silent. We can well imagine how deeply their ill-will hurt the heart of Jesus! He looked at them with anger. Hoping against hope to touch their hearts, Jesus cured the man, but He did it in a way that did not break the Sabbath, for He simply spoke saying, "Stretch out your hand." Speaking was not forbidden on the Sabbath.

This frontal attack on Sabbath-casuistry was the last straw. His cunning antagonists, these Pharisees, were roundly defeated. Nothing was left for them but to plot to kill Him.

Since Jesus happened to be in the territory of Herod, his sanction would be needed for any successful plot to kill Jesus. Therefore the Pharisees took counsel with the Herodians on how they might kill Jesus (*Mk.* 3:6). The Herodians were Herod supporters or persons of great influence in his court.

Chapter 4

Building the Kingdom, June-July, A.D. 28

Jesus' overtures to the religious leaders of Judaism had been in vain. Their response was to plot with the Herodians on how they might kill Him.

Jesus had tried to put the new wine of His teachings in old wineskins, but it did not succeed. So He withdrew to an area seven miles southwest of Capernaum to the Mount of the Beatitudes rising above the Plain of Gennesareth. From the mountaintop one can get one of the best views of the sea, stretching from Capernaum to Tiberias.

Today on the mountaintop there stands a beautiful chapel, the work of the architect Barluzzi. It is an octagonal building, to symbolize the eight beatitudes, one of which is inscribed on each of the windows. The chapel was completed in 1938.

THE FOUNDATION-STONES OF THE KINGDOM: THE TWELVE APOSTLES (Mk. 3:13-19; Lk. 6:12-16), JUNE, A.D. 28

It was now June or July, four months since Jesus' first disciples had come to Him down by the Jordan. His marvelous words and works, far from winning the religious leaders of the people, had only alienated them. Indeed, capital are the sins of envy and pride. St. Catherine of Siena, one of the two women doctors of the Church, exclaimed, "O cursed intellectualism, drier than dust without the tears of humility!"

The response of the plain, simple, ordinary folk, however, was far otherwise. Crowds bigger than ever followed

31

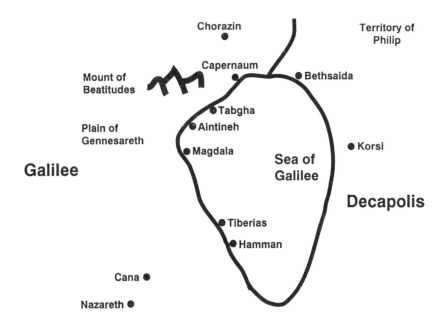

Jesus with enthusiasm. From them He intended to fashion new wineskins, to lay the foundation stones for His new spiritual edifice, the Church.

Before making this momentous choice, Jesus, as always, turned to prayer. Not only did He feel the need of His Father's help, but He also wished by example to teach His future Church leaders never to start anything of great importance without first praying. So He climbed a mountain and prayed all night (*Lk.* 6:12). At daybreak, from the vast throng, He called to Himself men of His own choosing. He did the calling. He did the choosing. Later, He would remind them, "You have not chosen me, I have chosen you."

And He chose twelve (whom He named apostles). For He was making a clean break with Judaism. His choice marked the parting of the ways between Judaism and Christianity.

The Twelve were to succeed the twelve tribes of Israel and were to form the new Israel.

He chose these Twelve, as St. Mark tells it, "that they might be with Him," to imbibe His spirit and to absorb His teachings, so that later *"He might send them forth to preach and to have authority to drive out demons"* (*Mk.* 3:14-15). St. Matthew adds that He gave them authority *"to cure every disease and every illness"* (*Mt.* 10:1), for Jesus was concerned about the whole person.

The Twelve consisted of three sets of brothers, all from Galilee with the exception of Judas. The gospels list them into three groups of four. Peter's name is always at the head of the first group: Peter, Andrew, James, and John. James, called the Great, and John were the first and last to be martyred. Philip heads the second list: Philip, Bartholomew, Thomas, and Matthew. And James, called the Less, the first bishop of Jerusalem, heads the third group: James, son of Alphaeus, Thaddeus (Jude), Simon the Cananean, and Judas Iscariot. James the Less is called the "brother of Christ," for Alphaeus was the brother of St. Joseph (the Hebrews called cousins "brothers"). He was martyred A.D. 62. Judas is always last.

With the exception of Matthew and Judas, the twelve were just ordinary people, industrious, patient, good-willed, and God-fearing. Jesus needed nothing more. *"He chose the foolish of the world to shame the wise, and He chose the weak of the world to shame the strong, and He chose the lowly and despised of the world, those who count for nothing, to reduce to nothing those who are something, so that no human being might boast before God"* (*1 Cor.* 1:27-29).

These twelve, next to Mary and Joseph, were to become the greatest in God's kingdom. They were great because they saw the truth and the goodness that Jesus was, and they clung to Him in the face of all opposition. It was not easy to follow Jesus, especially when most of the religious leaders of His day and most of the people were aligned against Him. Even His fellow Nazarenes thought Him mad.

But these down-to-earth fishermen saw the goodness in Jesus, His sincerity, His holiness; and because their hearts were good, they remained loyal to Him, no matter the cost. Later when He asked His Father to watch over them, He gave as His reason: "They believed in Me and stood by Me." In the Office of the Apostles Jesus repeats the same thing: "You are the men who stood by me in my time of trial."

That is all that true greatness is—to see the right and follow it, to behold the good and love it. Such would the twelve be, with the exception of Judas.

Gilbert K. Chesterton, reflecting on our jury system, wrote: "Our civilization has decided, very justly decided, that determining the guilt or innocence of men is a thing too important to be trusted to trained men. If it wishes for light upon that awful matter, it asks men who know no more about the law than I know, but who can feel the things that I felt in the jury box.

"When it wants a library catalogued, or the solar system discovered, or any trifle of that kind, it uses up its specialists.

"But when it wishes anything done that is really serious, it collects twelve of the ordinary men standing about. The same thing was done, if I remember right, by the founder of Christianity."

THE KINGDOM: THE SERMON ON THE MOUNT (Mt. 5:1-16), JUNE-JULY, A.D. 28

The choice of the 12 marked a parting of the ways between Judaism and Christianity. Heretofore, Jesus preached baptism and penance. In the Sermon on the Mount, Jesus made it clear how His teachings and doctrines were something totally distinct and new, needing new wine sacks.

After having chosen the twelve, Jesus came part way down the mountain with them. He sat down because a teacher sits, because the audience would be more relaxed, and so more receptive to learning, and because He was going to talk for a long period of time.

He was going to teach them that the goal of His kingdom is happiness; that its object is the whole world; and that its nature is from within, a matter of the heart in regard to law, the acts of religion, God's providence, and neighbor.

The Goal of the Kingdom: Happiness

The Beatitudes. If you are going to take a trip, do you not start at the end? Isn't your first thought about your destination: "Where am I going?" It makes all the difference in the world regarding your preparations to know whether you are going to Alaska or to Hawaii. In philosophy we say, "The end is first in the intention, but last in the execution." In war, victory is the first aim in the mind of a general, yet it is the last thing achieved.

So Jesus began His teaching on His kingdom with the Beatitudes, with happiness, to make it clear that happiness is the goal of the Christian life even though it may be the last thing you arrive at.

In the Beatitudes, Jesus laid down the blueprint for happiness. It is the exact opposite of what the world holds out as the way to happiness.

The world says—

Happy are the go-getters, they get on in the world.

Happy are the strong, they don't get pushed around.

Happy are the insensitive, nothing disturbs them.

Happy are the slave-drivers, they get results.

Happy are the sophisticated, they know their way around.

Happy are the trouble-makers, they make headlines.

Happy are those who go along, they get along.

The world posits happiness in **pleasures:** riches, honors, and sensuality.

Jesus said, "Happy are the poor in spirit, the meek, and those who weep for sin." The word "fun" comes from the medieval English "fon" meaning "fool." How often persons have found misery, not "fun" or "happiness," by pursuing only things.

The world focuses on **action:** loving and acting as you please, doing your own thing, getting all you can and keeping it.

Jesus said, "Happy are those who hunger for holiness and who are merciful." The rich man who planned to build bigger barns to hold his bountiful harvest and then rest, eat, drink, be merry, was called by Jesus "a fool" (*Lk.* 12:20).

Finally, the world thinks that **knowledge** gives happiness. Plato said the happy man is the wise man.

Jesus said that happiness is in the heart, not in the head; it is a reward, not a merit—a reward to the clean of heart and the peacemakers.

Of course Jesus' way will prompt persecution. Goodness pricks the conscience of the evildoer. *"Everyone who does wicked things hates the light . . ."* (*Jn.* 3:20). For this reason, Paul warned Timothy, *"All who want to live religiously in Christ Jesus will be persecuted"* (*2 Tm.* 3:12). If you walk with the wind at your back, you will hardly feel it. But if you walk into the wind, you will feel its bite. So those who walk with the devil do not feel his presence. But those who walk against him will taste his fury. Those who follow the path of the world will have a relatively easy time of it, for the world loves its own. But those who are not of the world, the world hates.

Therefore, one mark of the Christian is suffering. The goal is happiness. *Per aspera ad astra*—"Through bitter paths to the stars." *Per crucem ad lucem*—"Through the cross to the light." The great paradox: "Rejoice and be glad, for your reward will be great in heaven."

The Scope of the Kingdom: the World

Apostles, salt and light. The members of Jesus' kingdom must not only live the spirit of the Beatitudes, they must communicate this holiness to all mankind. Turning to His apostles, Jesus said, "You are the salt of the earth . . . . You are the light of the world." He used the terms "earth" and "world," because He meant His kingdom to reach out to all, not just to one nation, nor just to one people, but to everybody on earth, to the whole world. Jesus was a man for others, so He willed His followers to be. He wanted them to reflect His role: to be saviors of the world as He was. Faith is given to be shared with others.

Goodness, if it is present, has got to be felt like the pinch of salt on food.

Goodness, if it is present, has got to spread like the light that scatters darkness.

If it is not, then the salt loses its savor and the light is put under a bushel basket.

The salt that seasons the world is both the good flavor of a virtuous life, and the truth of the Gospel that prevents the corruption of error.

The light that scatters the darkness is good example, and the witnessing to the true, the good, and the beautiful.

In a word, Jesus wanted His disciples to change the quality of life around themselves by loving, giving, serving, by being kind, by doing all the good they can, wherever they can and whenever they can. Further, to do all this, not to be applauded by people nor to win God's love (He already loves us), but to draw others to our Father in Heaven.

A Christmas classic movie is Frank Capra's *"It's a Wonderful Life,"* with Donna Reed and Jimmy Stewart.

Stewart plays George Bailey in the small town of Bedford Falls. His father leaves him a Building and Loan Association. George gets into financial trouble. He thinks his life is a failure, so he goes to the town bridge toying with the idea of drowning himself.

Just before plunging into the icy waters, he says a short prayer. God answers his prayer, as Isaiah said He would, for those who help others as George had always done. God sends George's guardian angel, Clarence.

Clarence jumps into the river before George does. Clarence calls for help, and George, always ready to help others, reacts instinctively and jumps into the river and saves Clarence.

After their clothes have dried, Clarence takes George on a tour of Bedford Falls and shows him what the town and many of its people would have become had it not been for his helping hand. It is then that George realizes that all the help he had given people had redeemed countless lives and made Bedford Falls the wonderful town it was—all because George Bailey had lived there, being kind and helpful to others.

To climax it all, the people whom he had helped poured out their love to George when he was in need. Their outpouring of love moved George to tears and he cried out, "It's a wonderful life."

Similarly, Jesus calls His own to change the quality of life around themselves by being salt—seasoning society with their kindness and compassion; and by being light—radiating goodness and love to all. In this way they too shall find happiness and discover also that "It's a Wonderful Life."

The Nature of the Kingdom in Regard to Law
(*Mt.* 5:17-48)

Because Jesus often broke the Sabbath to do good, His enemies attacked Him as a scoffer of the law. To set the record straight, Jesus proclaimed: "Do not think that I have come to abolish the law . . . . I have come to fulfill" the law. By fulfilling the law, Jesus meant interiorizing it. Judaism had become a religion of legalism—just keeping laws. Laws regulate external actions, people's behavior, so that they can live together in harmony, get along. But laws leave the heart and mind of man untouched; they do not address motives and intentions. Thus a person can be law-abiding and yet be a despicable person, like Scrooge before his conversion in Dickens' *Christmas Carol*.

The scribes and the Pharisees were of that sort: they gloried in their keeping the law, but they were filled with pride, envy, greed. Jesus called them whited sepulchers, beautiful on the outside but full of dead bones on the inside. They offered lip-service to God, but their hearts were far from Him. In fact, Jesus warned His followers that unless their righteousness abounded more than that of the scribes and Pharisees they would not enter the kingdom of Heaven.

The heart of religion is the heart. Its goal is perfection. The key to obtaining perfection is the interior life: a life of love for Jesus and His way. Antoine de Saint-Exupery in his wonderful book *The Little Prince* has the fox give the Prince this secret: "It is only with the heart that one can see rightly; what is essential is invisible to the eye" (p. 70). If law is to sanctify, it must touch the heart. Thus David said, "Indeed you love truth in the heart." Three times a day, I pray David's prayer: *"A pure heart create for me, O God, put a steadfast spirit in me"* (*Ps.* 51:12). Jesus demanded that the heart be purified. *"From the heart come evil thoughts, murder, adultery . . ."* (*Mt.* 15:19).

And the heart is purified by doing all that we do out of love for God. It is not what we do that counts, but why; not the mountains we move, but the motives that impel us to move them. As the light of the body is the eye, so the light of religious acts is the good intention.

Jesus then exemplified what is meant by interiorizing the law. He took six commandments of the law. He introduced each with the words: "You have heard that it was said to your ancestors," or a similar formula; then He said, "But I say to you." Three commandments He accepted, but amplified, namely, the commandments regarding anger, adultery, and love of enemies. However, the three commandments regarding divorce, oaths, and retaliation, He rejected as standards of conduct for His disciples.

Thus in respect to the law, "Thou shalt not kill," Jesus extended it to include not only murder, but all that leads to murder: revenge, anger, abusive language, contempt of others. A heart filled with such venom is unfit to worship God. So Jesus commanded that one be reconciled with his brother before coming to the altar to worship God.

Jesus treated adultery the same way. He pointed out that the law includes more than the act of adultery. That of course is wrong. But Jesus went further and said that all other acts that adulterate the bloodstream of the human race and that pollute sex, which is the gateway to life, acts such as, the lascivious look, the X-rated thoughts and desires, pornography, salacious movies and novels that feed impure thoughts and desires, that eventually lead to the scarlet sin—all such acts are wrong.

As for divorce, Jesus said there is no such thing. To divorce and remarry is adultery plain and simple, "unless the marriage is unlawful," that is, was no marriage in the first place. In such a situation, one must either get married properly or separate.

Then Jesus extolled sincerity. He Himself was so sincere that He frowned not only on perjury but even on oath taking. He said, "Let your 'yes' mean 'yes' and your 'no' mean 'no,' and let it go at that." If a person's words were his bond, oaths would be obsolete. The father of lies is the devil.

Next, Jesus abrogated the *Lex Talionis,* the Law of the Claw: an eye for an eye and a tooth for a tooth. Before there were lawcourts, relatives would take the law into their own hands. More often than not, they would exceed the bounds of justice. For instance, Lamech killed a youth for bruising him (*Gn.* 4). When Shechem raped Dinah, Jacob's daughter, her brothers massacred all the men of the town and sacked the town in reprisal (*Gn.* 34).

The Law of the Claw insisted that the punishment must be in proportion to the crime, never in excess of it. And that was an improvement.

However, Jesus rejected even this tit-for-tat justice. He said, "If someone injures you, turn the other cheek." *"A mild answer breaketh wrath"* (*Prov.* 15:1).

By law a Roman soldier could impress anyone to carry his gear for a thousand footsteps (*mille pasuum,* from which we get our word "mile"). That happened to Simon of Cyrene. What a blessing it brought him! Jesus said that it was better to bear unjust laws, like that of Roman impressment, than to start a revolution. Love conquers all.

In other words, Jesus was giving His followers sound psychological advice: they were to be like Himself; they were always to retaliate with love; they were always to act in love, but never to be reactors—treating people as people treat them. Only in this way can the world be changed.

> I went out to find a friend,
> But could not find one there.
> I went out to be a friend,
> And friends were everywhere.

Then Jesus threw down the gauntlet: "Love your enemies, and pray for those who persecute you."

Why? Because that is the way God loves. God loves unconditionally; He loves even the unlovable. He doesn't discriminate. He lets His sun shine on the bad and the good alike and causes His rain to fall on both the just and the unjust. Only love like that would win people and beget friends.

Love may not make the world go round, but it sure makes life worth living, and obedience bearable and a joy.

By these six examples from the moral law of Moses, Jesus revealed the spirit of the law to His disciples, in order to wean them away from the corrupt interpretation of religion made by the scribes and the Pharisees.

The Nature of the Kingdom in Regard to the Great Works of Religion: Almsgiving, Prayer, and Fasting (*Mt.* 6:1-34)

The same principles that Jesus had applied to the law He now applied to the great works of religion. He said that praying, fasting, and giving alms for a wrong intention, doing them just to be seen by others, would render them worthless.

As one's destination determines direction, so one's intention in doing a work can enter into the determination of its goodness. Hence *"If your eye is bad, your whole body will be in darkness"* (*Mk.* 6:23).

How wonderfully Jesus exemplified these great works of religion in His life! His miracles could have made Him rich; but He did nothing for gain, only for love. He spent entire nights in prayer. As for fasting, His disciples often plucked grain from fields to allay their hunger. He worked miracles to feed the hungry, but never to feed Himself. His entire life was a giving; He left nothing for Himself. He could truly say, *"Foxes have dens and birds of the sky have nests, but the Son of Man has nowhere to rest his head"* (*Lk.* 9:58).

We can well imagine the impact His teachings on the works of religion must have had, for He practiced what He preached. Words move; examples convert.

Jesus endorsed almsgiving, for it is to fasting what rain is to the good earth; and He commended fasting, because it is the soul of prayer. Almsgiving makes virtue enduring; fasting makes devotion constant; and prayer makes faith firm. Prayer knocks at the door; fasting opens it; and almsgiving receives. Prayer accompanied by fasting and almsgiving gains all it asks for from God. In the Old Testament, prayer rescued the three young men in the fiery furnace. Prayer saved Daniel in a den of lions. Prayer brought down fire from heaven for Elijah.

Prayer can move God, can convert sinners, strengthen the weak, heal the sick, vanquish temptation, comfort the faint-hearted, lift up the fallen, support the falling, and keep the firm standing on their feet. St. Alphonsus Liguori said that if he had only one sermon to preach, it would be on prayer. Pray and you'll be saved; do not pray and you'll be lost.

But one thing Jesus taught again and again about praying is that you must persevere. "Ask and it will be given to you; seek and you will find; knock and the door will be opened to you." If at first you don't succeed, try and try again: ask, seek, knock!

To those tempted to give up on praying, Jesus tenderly reminded them that prayer is addressed to God who is a Father. He taught them to pray "Our Father in Heaven." Then with His usual irrefutable logic, Jesus asked, *"If an earthly father would not give his son a snake when he asks for a fish, or a stone when he asks for bread, how much more will your Father in heaven, who loves you more than any earthly father, give good things to those who ask Him?"* (*Mt.* 7:7-11).

To sum up, Jesus said in effect, "Never spoil these three great works of religion by doing them to be praised by men. Have your mind and heart set not on the things of this world but on the world beyond. *Do not store up for yourselves treasures on earth, where moth and decay destroy, and thieves break in and steal. But store up treasures in Heaven, where neither moth nor decay destroys, nor thieves break in and steal"* (Mt. 6:19-20).

The Nature of the Kingdom in Regard to God's Providence (*Mt.* 6:24-34)

So many do not pray, nor fast, nor give alms to others, because they depend too much on their own resources. It is significant that the Mother of God said to Jelena, one of the locutionists at Medjugorje: "Each Thursday, read again the passage of Matthew 6:24-34" (3/1/84).

Even in Jesus' day worry was a problem. It still is. Modern man has an anxiety complex! There is no doubt about it. An increasing number of persons are afflicted with neuroses, fears, frustrations, and ulcers. Many are so "run down" because they are so "wound up."

In yesteryears, people were anxious about their souls. Modern anxiety is principally about the body: economic security, health, complexion, social prestige, and so on.

The basis of much anxiety is trying to serve two masters: God and money. Man must choose one or the other. One choice will bring love, the other hate; one hope, the other despair. Trying to serve both is like tuning in on two radio stations at the same time—all you'll get is cacophony.

Jesus insisted that we must stop worrying over "What are we to eat, or what are we to drink . . . to wear?"

"Oh sure," you retort, "that's easy for Jesus to say. But who's going to pay the bills?"

Jesus didn't say, "Stop working!" He said, "Stop worrying! Don't be excessively anxious about your livelihood. Don't let the stress and strain of living take over. Do your best, and God your Father will do the rest."

Fill the water pots; He'll change the water into wine. Sow the seeds; He'll make them sprout. Work hard; He'll see you through.

Jesus reminded us that if God feeds the birds of the air and clothes the lilies of the field and the short-lived grass, how much more will He care for us! A robin and a sparrow were flying over a city at the noon hour. Seeing the crowds below hurrying and scurrying, worrying and flurrying:

> Said the robin to the sparrow,
> "Sparrow, I would like to know
> Why these human beings
> Rush about and worry so?"
>
> Said the sparrow to the robin,
> "Robin, I think that it must be
> They have no heavenly Father
> Such as cares for you and me."

Unable to continue his studies at Yale, William Cullen Bryant turned to law, though his heart was bent on a literary career. Forlorn and desolate, he walked from Cummington to Plainfield, Massachusetts, where he hoped to start his Law practice.

It was a winter's evening, but the western heavens were fired with warmth. Walking alone, he lifted his eyes and saw a solitary bird winging its way homeward across the pathless sky. He became glad, for he felt a kinship with the bird. In Bryant's troubled breast there gradually settled a calm confidence in the providence of God.

When he reached home, Bryant wrote his lovely poem, "To a Waterfowl."

> There is a Power whose care
> Teaches thy way along that
>   pathless coast—
> The desert and illimitable air—
> Lone, wandering, but not lost.
>
> He who, from zone to zone,

Guides through the boundless sky
thy certain flight,
In the long way that I must trod alone,
Will lead my steps aright.

A waterfowl inspired Bryant to see that there is "a divinity that shapes our ends, rough hew them how we will." And he regained hope. All Jesus asks of His own is, *"Trust in God and trust in me!"* (*Jn.* 14:1).

The Nature of the Kingdom in Regard to Our Neighbor: No Rash Judgments (*Mt.* 7:1-5)

From the very beginning of His public life, the scribes and Pharisees had been misjudging Jesus.

A rash judgment is jumping to conclusions about people. Jesus said, "Don't do that!" We cannot be judges, for we cannot see the human heart. Man sees appearances; only God can see the heart. Ben Johnson said, "God defers His judgment till Judgment Day. Let us do likewise."

It is great wisdom to give everyone the benefit of the doubt. You may be mistaken. But ten thousand mistakes are better than one sin of rash judgment.

During World War II, a company of American soldiers was charging an enemy position. An officer, standing in the line of attack, saw one of his men retreating from the scene of action. Interpreting his retreat as cowardice, the officer in anger ran over to the soldier and hit him with the butt end of his pistol. The soldier fell on his back. The officer, in the semi-darkness, saw the blood welling from a bullet hole in the soldier's chest. The wounded man looked up at the officer and whispered, "I was just looking for a place to die."

Though Jesus never wanted us to judge others, He still expected us to be discerning. Judgment is passing sentence on a person. That is a no-no. Discernment is passing judgment on whether or not to do something. That is common sense. Hence Jesus said, "Do not give that which is holy to dogs, to those who fight what is good and true, viciously and brutally. Nor throw pearls before swine, before those who are gross and stupid and scorn every overture to follow the good, as the worldly-minded do." Instead, He said, follow the golden rule: "Do to others whatever you would have them do to you."

Exhortation to Vigilance (*Mt.* 7:13-27)

Finally, Jesus pointed out that the kingdom of Heaven requires effort. First of all, it demands a hard, painstaking search, for the way is narrow—"The road is broad that leads to destruction . . . How narrow the gate . . . that leads to life."

In her Diary Sr. Faustina wrote:

"I saw two roads. One was broad, covered with sand and flowers, full of joy, music and all sorts of pleasures. People walked along it, dancing and enjoying themselves. They reached the end without realizing it. At the end of the road there was a horrible precipice; that is, the abyss of hell. The souls fell blindly into it; as they walked, so they fell. And their number was so great that it was impossible to count them.

"And I saw the other road, a path, for it was narrow and strewn with thorns and rocks; and the people who walked along it had tears in their eyes, and all kinds of suffering befell them. Some fell down upon the rocks, but stood up immediately and went on. At the end of the road there was a magnificent garden filled with all sorts of happiness, and all these souls entered there. At the very first instant they forgot all their sufferings" (p. 86).

Then further complicating making the right choice, Jesus warned against false prophets. "Test them," He advised, "by their fruits."

Finally, there is self-deception: mistaking talk for action—"Not everyone who says to me, 'Lord, Lord' will enter the kingdom of Heaven, but only the one who does the will of my Father in Heaven."

Remember Eliza Doolittle's song "Show Me," which she sang to Freddie in *My Fair Lady.*

> Words! Words! Words!
> I'm so sick of words! . . .
> Don't talk of stars burning above;
> If you're in love,
> Show me!

Sing me no song!	Don't talk of June!
Read me no rhyme!	Don't talk of fall!
Don't waste my time,	Don't talk at all!
Show me!	Show me!

Jesus also said that it will take more than words to enter the kingdom of Heaven. Therefore, Jesus concluded: we must not only listen to Him; we must also do as He says. No point going to a doctor unless we are prepared to do as he says. "Everyone who listens to my words and acts on them will be like a wise man who built his house on rock." Thus, when the rains of temptation, and the floods of persecution, and the winds of opposition buffet him, he will not collapse for he has built his house solidly on rock.

But the listener who does not act on His words will be like a fool who built his house in a wadi, a dried-up river bed. When the winds blow and the rains fall, and the wadi becomes a raging torrent, his house will be washed away. Jesus knew what He was talking about for He was a master builder.

St. James put it this way: *"If anyone is a hearer of the*

word and not a doer he is like a man who looks at his own face in a mirror. He sees himself, then goes off and promptly forgets what he looked like" (1:23-24).

When Jesus had finished, the crowds were astonished at his teaching and at the way He taught, for He taught them as one having authority, not as the scribes. Moses said one thing; Jesus dared to say another.

The Sermon on the Mount was simply a description of what Jesus and John the Baptist meant by repentance (the Greek word is *metanoia,* meaning "a change of heart and mind"). It stated clearly and forcefully the new spirit that must animate those who would enter the kingdom of Heaven.

July-October
A.D. 28

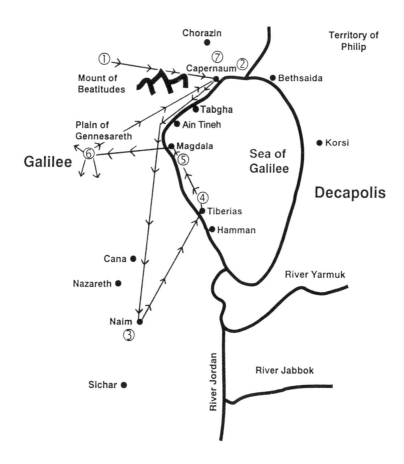

① To Capernaum
② July: Jesus heals centurion's servant
③ July: Jesus raises young man from death at Naim
④ August: Testimony regarding the Baptist
⑤ September: Forgives Mary Magdalene
⑥ October: Tours Galilee, Galilean women follow
　　From one town and village Jesus proclaims good news (*Lk.* 8:1).
⑦ At Capernaum relatives upset

Chapter 5

Training the Twelve, July-October, A.D. 28

Jesus ended the Sermon on the Mount with the exhortation to act on His teachings. Following His own advice, Jesus followed His sermon with actions: He preached to the people and healed their sick and their possessed. He wished to give His apostles very concrete demonstrations of just what He expected them to do when they would become His emissaries.

A PAGAN CENTURION, JULY, A.D. 28 (*Lk.* 7:1-10)

After the Sermon on the Mount, Jesus returned to Capernaum. The elders of the Jews came to Him and entreated Him to go to the home of a Roman centurion and heal his servant who was on the point of death. Jesus went. When the centurion learned of this, he sent other friends to Jesus saying, *"Lord, do not trouble yourself, I am not worthy to have you enter under my roof . . . I'm a man of authority: I say to one 'Go,' and he goes, to another 'Come,' and he comes, so say but the word and let my servant be healed."*

Jesus marveled at the man and said, *"Not even in Israel have I found such faith."* In reward for such faith, He healed the servant and willed that the centurion's words become immortalized in every Mass—a fitting tribute to the man who built the synagogue in Capernaum where Jesus would promise the Eucharist ten months later.

THE NAIMITES, JULY, A.D. 28 (*Lk.* 7:11-17)

After this incident, Jesus left Capernaum to continue His

evangelization of Galilee. This missionary tour lasted to the end of August. During it, He came to the town of Naim, thirty miles southwest of Capernaum, and five miles southeast of Nazareth.

In Arabic the word "naim" means "sleep." Maybe Naim was a "sleepy hollow" kind of village. Here a young man was asleep in death; he was being carried to the cemetery. He was an only son. Jesus pitied the widowed mother. So He stopped the cortege and raised the lad from the dead; then with profound consideration, Jesus returned him to his widowed mother.

This was the first miracle of this kind. News of it spread like wildfire throughout the whole of Judea and in all the surrounding region. Jesus seized the opportunity to preach and teach in the area; He backtracked to the lakeside cities and consolidated His gains.

JOHN THE BAPTIST, AUGUST, A.D. 28 (*Mt.* 11:2-6)

Even John, now four months in prison at Macherus about a hundred miles from where Jesus was, heard of His raising the widow of Naim's son from the dead. Because Jesus' disciples did not fast, because Jesus Himself lacked the fire and thunder of the Baptist, some of the Baptist's disciples had doubts about Jesus' Messiahship. To dispel their doubts, John sent two of his disciples to Jesus at the lakeside.

Jesus catalogued His works for them: "the blind see, the lame walk, the lepers are cleansed, the deaf hear, the dead are raised, and the poor have the good news proclaimed to them." He came as Isaiah the prophet foretold: *"Not crying out, not shouting, not making his voice heard in the street. A bruised reed he shall not break, and a smoldering wick he shall not quench"* (42:2-3). In other words, Jesus explained to them how He was fulfilling God's prophetic plan for the Kingdom: it must grow slowly, without fanfare and outward show. He warned them not to disbelieve. The disciples left and reported their interview to John.

When they had gone, Jesus turned to the crowd and eulogized John. The questions of John's disciples might have created the impression that John himself was wavering about whether Jesus was the one who is to come. Jesus dispelled these impressions by saying that John was no reed shaken by the wind, no sycophant dressed in fine clothing. In fact, of all the Old Testament prophets, Jesus said none was greater than John.

THE CROWDS AND THE PHARISEES, SEPTEMBER, A.D. 28 (*Mt.* 11:7-19)

As Jesus was speaking, He saw the crowds jostling, pushing, shoving, struggling to get closer to Him to hear His every word. It seemed to Jesus as if the kingdom of Heaven was being assaulted and seized by force—"the kingdom of Heaven suffers violence, and the violent are taking it by force."

However, on the fringe of the crowd, Jesus noticed the haughty Pharisees, looking with contempt on the crowd, standing aloof, smug, complacent, confident as though they had no need of reform. Shaking His head, Jesus likened them to kids who would not join the other kids in playing games. For them, John was too strict and Jesus too lenient. They refused to play God's game; whereas the poor and the lowly were willing and thus were entering the kingdom.

A PHARISEE AND A SINFUL WOMAN, SEPTEMBER, A.D. 28 (*Lk.* 7:36-50)

Going along the lake coast, Jesus came to Magdala. The Pharisees in Galilee were not so antagonistic to Jesus as those from Jerusalem. His popularity demanded that He be accorded some recognition. At Magdala, there lived a Pharisee, Simon, a bit sympathetic toward Jesus, who invited Him to dinner. However, there was a certain coolness in his welcome, for he omitted the ordinary acts of courtesy.

A sinful woman, Mary Magdalene, compensated for the rudeness by herself washing the feet of Jesus and anointing Him. Jesus in turn graciously reprimanded Simon and then vindicated the woman, making known that her sins had been forgiven. (See Note at the end of the chapter.)

Sinners were entering the kingdom; whereas the self-satisfied Pharisees remained outside. *"The hungry he has filled with good things; the rich he has sent away empty"* (*Lk.* 1:53).

FRIENDS AND RELATIVES, OCTOBER, A.D. 28 (*Lk.* 8:1-3; *Mk.* 3:31-35)

Jesus continued His mission for some length of time, going through the towns and villages of Galilee, proclaiming the good news of the kingdom. During the hot, dry summer months, He could have easily slept outdoors, gotten along without shelter—but not without food and garments. Certain women, whom Jesus had helped, like Mary Magdalene, Joanna, the wife of Chuza, Herod's steward, and Susanna, supplied those needs.

His relatives from Nazareth, on the contrary, reacted differently. When He had returned to Capernaum, they were there to try to put a stop to His foolishness. They thought He had lost His mind. *"A prophet is not without honor except . . . among his own kin"* (*Mk.* 6:4). Though Mary was with them, she did not share their sentiments; she was there ready to defend Him if need be!

When Jesus learned of this, He looked at those around Him, and with indescribable majesty, He stretched out His hands and said, *"My mother and brothers are all those who hear the word of God and keep it."* For Jesus, membership in His kingdom transcended all the limitations of blood relationship; it included anyone who does the will of God.

Note

Mary Magdalene. Tradition identifies the sinful woman of Luke's gospel who washes the feet of Jesus (*Lk.* 7:37) with Mary Magdalene and Mary of Bethany. All three women are one.

Magdala was less than three miles from Tiberias. Herod Antipas had built the city in honor of Tiberias Caesar around A.D. 20. Besides his luxurious palace there, the city boasted of an arena that could seat 10,000 spectators, and hot springs that made it a resort for the rich. Its magnificence and wealth attracted the vivacious, fascinating, good-looking Mary from nearby Magdala. Befriended by Joanna, the wife of Chuza, Herod's steward, she entered Herod's court, and was soon seduced by its luxury and pleasures.

Mary Magdalene was not a street prostitute. She was a court courtesan, richly attired, impeccably groomed, associate of men of high rank, and seen publicly with them at official functions. Hence her reputation as a sinner.

She was wealthy—her precious spikenard poured on the feet of Jesus would have cost a workingman his year's pay. Outrageously demonstrative, she undid her long, magnificent tresses to wipe the feet of Jesus as her bitter tears mingled with the perfumed oil. Her tears admitted guilt. She knew her sins, and so did He whose feet she embraced.

Both Magdala and Tiberias were on the road Jesus often took back and forth from Capernaum and Judea. Probably on one of those occasions, Mary, in company with Joanna, heard Jesus preach. Both of them raved so to Herod that *"he was anxious to meet Jesus"* (*Lk.* 9:7-9). Mary, however, was more than curious; she was so touched that she went to Jesus, as He dined at the house of Simon.

Simon was scandalized, but not Jesus. Moved by her tears and her anointing, the great heart of Jesus forgave the sinner and sent her away in peace. Later, she and Joanna and other women accompanied Jesus and ministered to Him on His journeys (*Lk.* 8:2-3).

Whenever Jesus went to Jerusalem, He made Bethany, the home of Mary Magdalene, Martha and Lazarus, His headquarters.

In the sixth century Pope St. Gregory the Great proclaimed: "We believe that the one that Luke calls a sinner, that John names 'Mary' is the same out of whom, according to Mark, 'seven demons were expelled.' " Before him, St. Jerome and Origen said the same thing. In fact, up to the 15th century the sinner in Luke's gospel, Mary Magdalene, and Mary of Bethany were always thought to be one and the same person.

But in every age a number of critics arise who refute old beliefs and introduce new theories in the interpretation of Scriptures. They usually manage to stir up controversy, divide opinions, and often leave the Christian world the poorer for it.

This happened in the 15th century. New opinions about Mary Magdalene arose. Some divided her into two distinct women: Mary Magdalene and Mary of Bethany; or even into three: the sinner and the two Marys. Is it not strange we hear nothing of "Mary of Bethany"—only of Mary Magdalene? That we have feasts for Martha and Mary Magdalene and none for Mary of Bethany?

Jesus took a despised sinner to show God is above the petty judgments of men; and He glorified her, because she had loved more than all others and because He wished to show the transforming power of love. *Amor vincit omnia:* "Love conquers all things."

> (Fillette, Edith. *Saint Mary Magdalene.*
> Society of Saint Mary Magdalene, Box 18,
> Newton Lower Falls, Massachusetts 02162.)

Parables in November followed by miracles in December

① Jesus crosses sea—calms storm
② Jesus cures the demoniac at Korsi
③ At Capernaum—heals woman with hemorrhage
  —raises Jairus' daughter
  —cures two blind and dumb demoniacs
④ Second visit to Nazareth
⑤ Jesus went around to all the towns and villages
  (January-March 29) then returns to Capernaum.

Chapter 6

The Parables of the Kingdom

EIGHT PARABLES ABOUT THE KINGDOM, NOVEMBER, A.D. 28 (*Mt.* 13:1-53; *Mark* 4:26-29)

As the hostility of the Pharisees intensified and their influence increased, Jesus changed His teaching methods by using the parable.

A parable is just a short story, taken from everyday life, to illustrate a truth. Thus parables have two sides: the story side, which is obvious; and the message side, which is not so obvious. Like chiaroscouro in painting, parables have light and shadow. The light side, the story, entertains and captures attention; the shadow side, the lesson of the story, stimulates curiosity. The well-disposed generally discover the point of the parable, but the ill-disposed, like the Pharisees, miss it altogether. Thus God in His mercy can diminish their culpability.

Jesus used a series of parables to teach His followers that His kingdom would ultimately succeed despite all obstacles. Jesus probably spoke these parables down by the seaside, between Ain Tineh and Tabgha. The fact He delivered His parables at the seashore, and not in the synagogue of Capernaum, gives some indication of how strong the opposition against Him had become.

Four of these parables deal with the sowing of crops. It was probably November, when farmers in Palestine began to sow the wheat and barley crops after the first autumn rains. It could be that Jesus saw a farmer actually sowing seed.

Generally, we ought not allegorize a parable; that is, make every detail in the story stand for something else. Normally, a parable has one lesson. An easy way to get at the lesson is to use the comparative words: **"Just as . . . so too."**

The Parable of the Sower and the Seed (*Mt.* 13:1-9)

The fact that Jewish religious leaders sought to kill Jesus tended to depress and discourage the apostles. To bolster their hope, Jesus told them the parable of the Sower and the Seed.

Fields in those days had no hedges. Stony or hard-trodden paths bordered them. As Jesus watched the farmer sowing seed, He said, "Behold, the sower went out to sow . . . ." Then He told a story about the seed falling on different kinds of soil.

The first point He wanted to make was that **just as** the farmer has a great harvest regardless of the loss of some of the seed, **so too** the kingdom of God would prosper no matter the losses or opposition. In the parable, Jesus also showed from where the losses and opposition would come.

First, it would stem from those persons hardened by intellectual pride, egoism, and a sense of self-sufficiency. The I-don't-need-God type. These are easy prey to the devil who plucks from their hearts the least glimmerings of grace (the footpath and the birds).

The next group are those persons who are fair-weather Christians, sunshine soldiers and summer patriots; that is, they stay with the Church as long as things go their way. But let problems arise or let their minds and wills be crossed and they wither away, fall by the wayside (the rocky soil).

Finally, there are the busy-busy people, the people so engaged in being successful in this world, in making money, a name, or fame, they have no time for God (the thorns). The world is everything to them.

The point Jesus wanted to make was that these lapses must not discourage, because in spite of these losses, the kingdom would be enormously successful. In the end there will be so abundant a harvest that it will far surpass any and all the losses. Hence there is cause only for hope.

The Parable of the Growth of the Seed (*Mk.* 4:26-29)

Just as the seed grows of itself, first the blade, then the ear, then the full grain, **so too** God's Kingdom will grow silently but surely, slowly but powerfully, without human intervention. One must be patient, confident.

The Parable of the Wheat and the Weeds
(*Mt.* 13:24-30)

Just as one's enemy might sow weeds among the wheat, **so too** the enemy of all mankind will cause some to sin and intermingle with the good in the kingdom. However, **just as** in the harvest time, the weeds will be separated from the wheat, so **too** in the judgment the bad will be separated from the good.

Until then, Jesus warned His followers not to anticipate the final judgment of God by a definitive exclusion of sinners from the kingdom. God's judgment will do that. Instead, they are to be patient and to preach repentance.

The Parable of the Mustard Seed (*Mt.* 13:31-32)

The smallness of the mustard seed was proverbial in Palestine: "Tiny as a mustard seed," they say. Yet the seed sprouts into a tree ten feet tall and all the birds of the air dwell among its branches. **Just as** the mustard seed is tiny in the beginning but large in the end, **so too** God's kingdom begins small, but it will grow and grow until it embraces all the nations of the world. Again, Jesus asks for patience, because it takes a lot of slow to grow.

The Parable of the Yeast (*Mt.* 13:33)

Jesus spoke of three measures or forty quarts, an enormous amount, enough to feed a hundred people. This element is exaggerated to point out the greatness of the effect of the kingdom. **Just as** a little yeast makes a whole batch of dough tasty, **so too** God's kingdom will permeate and penetrate all society, sanctifying it and begetting Christian civilization. Pope Paul VI said, that "the mission of the Church is to create a civilization of love."

The Parables of the Treasure and the Pearl (*Mt.* 13:44-46)

Just as a man seeks and searches for a field with a treasure hidden in it or a priceless pearl, and will spend all to buy these, **so too** one must seek and search for God's kingdom and give all to possess it, for what it has to give exceeds all worldly possessions. It is significant that the devil offered Jesus all the kingdoms of the world for His immortal soul.

As the treasure and the pearl were eventually found, so the earnest seeker after the kingdom most assuredly will find it. And once he has found it, he rarely will relinquish it, because of the great inner peace and joy it brings.

The Parable of the Net (*Mt.* 13:47-50)

This parable has the same message as that of the wheat and the weeds.

Just as a net snares all kinds of fish, good and bad, which are separated on the shore, **so too** in the kingdom there will be good and bad alike, to be separated finally on the shores of eternity. Hence the need for tolerance.

Jesus concluded these parables with the observation that the Old Testament is not to be neglected. Just as new insights regarding the kingdom can be drawn from old, familiar stories (like parables), so the apostles and their successors from the teachings of Jesus are to discover in the old teachings of Israel, that which is new.

Therefore Jesus urged His apostles to be like the head of a household and bring out of the storehouse of revelation things both old and new; in other words, to show how the law and the prophets were but a preparation for the coming of Jesus, that in Him they found their fulfillment. This would better dispose the Jews to receive His kingdom and become members of it.

St. Mark puts the parables of the kingdom after five conflict stories between Jesus and the scribes and Pharisees. He wanted to show that the kingdom would be victorious in the end, regardless of the opposition and obstacles.

". . . When seed is sown in a field, very much is certain to be lost; but, equally, much will fall on good ground and will produce a harvest, and a great one, some of it of the highest quality. Again, a lamp is intended and destined to give forth its light, not to be obscured and useless. If treasure has to be hidden for a time, it is only in order that it may some day be revealed; it does not remain concealed forever. Again, we all know that a farmer has labors and troubles in plenty; he must plough, harrow and weed; and no doubt many dangers—bad weather, insects, disease—all threaten the seed; but if he is wise, he will not be consumed with daily anxiety about the growth of his crop; the earth of its own accord—or, if we prefer it, God—will give the silent, mysterious, all-important increase, ending or culminating in the harvest. And finally a mustard seed, if the principle of life is in it, even though it be so small that we can hardly see it, will in due course produce a great bush.

"The same note runs throughout; final success in spite of temporary hindrance; if a work or purpose be of God it cannot be defeated; rather, the temporary hindrance has its part to play . . ." (R. H. Lightfoot, *The Gospel Message of St. Mark,* p. 40).

THE FUTURE GROWTH OF THE KINGDOM

The Kingdom will grow despite all opposition, because of the infinite power of Jesus, which He demonstrates to His apostles by a series of tremendous miracles, Dec. A.D. 28.

The Storm on the Sea, December, A.D. 28
(*Mk.* 4:35-40)

After His discourse on the parables, Jesus took the apostles across the sea. He wanted to let them see the magnitude of His power. They were to fear neither human enemies nor diabolical ones.

Very likely, the apostles, like the Galilean crowds, were getting their false Messianic hopes up again. They needed more time with Him alone. Moreover, Jesus was exhausted, so He said, "Let us cross to the other side"—to the eastern shore of the Sea. It seemed that this was a spur-of-the-moment decision, for "they took him with them in the boat just as he was."

Humbly, Jesus obeyed their orders. They put Him in the stern of the boat so He would be out of the way, for He was a carpenter, no fisherman. So tired was He that He fell fast asleep. Other boats were with them, but a sudden, violent squall dispersed them and terrified the seasoned fishermen, though it did not awaken the weary-worn Jesus.

Thoroughly frightened, the apostles in desperation awoke Jesus, crying out, "Teacher, do you not care that we are perishing?" Rising, Jesus rebuked the winds and the waves and a great calm came. Then He asked them, "Why are you terrified? Do you not yet have faith?" His power awed them; they wondered, "Who is this whom even the wind and sea obey?"

The Healing of the Demoniacs, December,
A.D. 28 (*Mk.* 5:1-20)

After the storm had subsided, the apostles probably spent the rest of the night fishing. In the morning they landed on the eastern shore near Gerasa (modern Korsi) in the territory of the Gerasenes.

A demoniac spotted them. He was fearsome, wore no clothing, dwelt in the hillside caves and not even chains could restrain him. Seeing Jesus, he cried out, "What have you to do with me, Jesus, Son of the Most High God?"

Jesus asked, "What is your name?" To impress the people, maybe even Jesus, he said his name was "Legion"—the Roman Legion was the terror and abomination of the Jews. Then he said, "Send us unto the swine"—they hoped that the destruction of the swine would turn the people of the district against Jesus. They were right; when the swine were destroyed, the people did entreat Jesus to leave their district. Jesus acceded, but He left behind the demoniac whom He had cured to herald the good news, and the cured man did proclaim in Decopolis all that Jesus had done.

The Woman With the Hemorrhage and Jairus' Daughter, Dec. A.D. 28 (*Mk.* 5:21-43)

Perhaps on the very same day He cured the demoniac, Jesus returned to Capernaum. Unlike the Gerasenes, the people of Capernaum eagerly awaited Him. For the third time, a notable of the city came to Jesus for help, a ruler of the synagogue named Jairus. His daughter of twelve was dying. Jairus begged Jesus to come and lay hands on her. Jesus followed him, but at a slow pace because the people were crowding Him.

A woman suffering for twelve years from a hemorrhage believed that if she could but touch the tassel on Jesus' cloak, she would be healed. She had spent all her money on physicians, seeking a cure, but in vain. So she drew up behind Jesus stealthily, for had the crowd known of her condition, they would have driven her away. She touched the hem of His garment and instantly the malady left her.

Jesus stopped and exposed the woman—not to embarrass

her, but that Jairus might catch something of her faith, for his faith was weak. He had demanded Jesus' physical presence for a cure. Moreover, when news came of his daughter's death, while Jesus was delayed by the woman, his friends said, "Why trouble the teacher any longer?" Their faith too was weak.

Jesus' response to Jairus was "Do not be afraid; just have faith." Jairus, having caught something of the woman's faith, believed. In response, Jesus raised the little girl from the dead. Mark gives a little touch about the compassion of Jesus. In the excitement about the miracle, no one thought of the little girl, except Jesus. It was He who told them to give her something to eat.

Two Blind Men and a Dumb Demoniac (*Mt.* 9:27-34)

News of this tremendous miracle spread throughout all that land (*Mt.* 9:26). Two blind men, they paired up for security, heard of this. So they accosted Jesus, as He passed on from there, crying out, "Son of David, have pity on us!" That was a Messianic title. Had Jesus cured them on the streets, the volatile Galileans might have risen then and there against Rome. So Jesus cured them only after He had reached the house where He was staying in Capernaum; but He sternly warned them to tell no one. Of course, they paid no attention; they were so elated at the recovery of their sight that they told everyone.

As they were going out peddling the news of their cure, a demoniac who could not speak was brought to Him. He cured him. But here again, there was a negative reaction. The Pharisees said, "He drives out demons by the prince of demons." So Jesus left Capernaum and headed for Nazareth.

Nazareth, December, A.D. 28
(*Mk.* 6:1-6; *Lk.* 4:22-30)

This was Jesus' second visit to Nazareth, about seven

months after His first. In the meanwhile He had preached and worked many miracles throughout Galilee. Also, He had located His headquarters at Capernaum, because it was the hub of traffic in the Middle East. All this did not set well with the Nazarenes. They resented His working miracles everywhere and not in Nazareth. They resented His slighting Nazareth for Capernaum. Then, too, envy made it hard for some to acknowledge one of their own—"the carpenter, the Son of Mary"—as their superior and teacher.

So when He returned this second time, His fellow-townsmen not only rejected Him, they actually sought to kill Him, to throw Him headlong over the brow of the hill on which Nazareth was built.

Some identify this hill with the Hill of the Precipice two miles south of Nazareth. Near there, in the Middle Ages, a chapel was built to commemorate Mary's terror at seeing her Son's life threatened. The chapel is called Our Lady of the Spasm. However, it is more probable that the precipice was in the northwestern part of Nazareth behind the present Maronite church. But Jesus left unharmed, amazed at their lack of faith.

ON-THE-JOB TRAINING FOR THE LEADERS-TO-BE OF THE KINGDOM, MARCH, A.D. 29

Commissioning the Twelve (*Mt.* 9:35-38; *Mk.* 6:6-7)

After Jesus had left Nazareth, He *"went around to all the towns and villages, teaching in their synagogues, proclaiming the gospel of the kingdom, and curing every disease and illness"* (*Mt.* 9:35).

Josephus said there were 204 towns and villages in Galilee with a population totaling about three million. In those months, from January to March, Jesus saw that the people were like sheep without a shepherd, because their spiritual leaders had failed them. He was moved to compassion. The harvest was vast and ripe, the people were ready for the Gospel, but He was only one person.

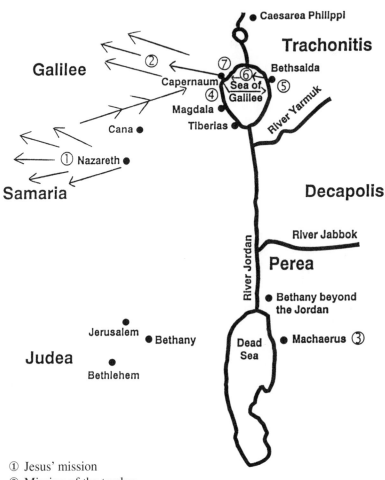

March-April
A.D. 29

Caesarea Phillppi

Trachonitis

Galilee ② Bethsalda

Capernaum ⑦ ⑥ Sea of Galilee ⑤

④

Magdala

Cana Tiberias River Yarmuk

① Nazareth

Samaria Decapolis

River Jabbok

River Jordan Perea

Bethany beyond the Jordan

Jerusalem Bethany Dead Sea Machaerus ③

Judea Bethlehem

① Jesus' mission
② Mission of the twelve
③ Martyrdom of John the Baptist
④ Return of the twelve to Capernaum
⑤ The miracle of the loaves and fish
⑥ Jesus walks on water
⑦ Promise of the Eucharist

So when He got back to Capernaum, He decided to send out His apostles to help reap the harvest. They had been with Him nine months. This would be good training for their future work. So He sent them out two by two to preach the good news and to heal the sick and cast out devils.

Instructions for Their Mission
(*Mt.* 10:5-16; *Mk.* 6:8-13)

Before sending them forth, however, Jesus instructed them. He told them where to go: to the lost sheep of Israel, not to the Gentiles or to the Samaritans—they were not ready to evangelize the Gentiles. He told them what to do: they were to preach that the the kingdom of God was at hand, and to cure the sick and drive out devils. He told them what they were to take with them: nothing but the clothes on their backs—they were to trust God totally. He told them where to stay: not at the inns, for people lodged there generally only for a night. They were to get to know the people. And the best way to do that was to stay at people's homes.

Finally, He told them how to behave: if people received them, they were to bless them; if not, they were to shake the dust of that town from their feet. They were never to retaliate violently, even if rejected or persecuted. This will happen, for evil people can be vicious, like wolves in sheep's clothing. The only defense of the good is to be wise, like a serpent, that slithers away at the slightest sign of attack, and innocent, like a dove, so as to give enemies no provocation.

The Martyrdom of John the Baptist, March, A.D. 29
(*Mt.* 14:6-12; *Mk.* 6:21-29)

John began his ministry in the desert about October, A.D. 27. He was imprisoned in about May, A.D. 28. Jesus eulogized him around September, A.D. 28. And Herod beheaded him in March, A.D. 29, at Macherus.

The occasion for John's execution was Herod's birthday party at Macherus. Herod Antipas was the son of Herod the

Great. When Herod the Great died in 4 B.C., young Herod Antipas became tetrarch of Galilee and Perea, which he had been ruling for thirty-two years. Even though he was married, he took Herodias, the wife of his half-brother, Herod Philip I, a union forbidden by *Leviticus* 18:16. Philip was the tetrarch of Iturea and Trachonitis. John the Baptist had denounced this adulterous and incestuous marriage and had thus incurred the enmity of both Herod and Herodias. (See Note at end of chapter.)

At Herod's birthday party, Herodias' fifteen year old daughter, Salome, danced lasciviously for Herod's guests. He was so pleased, he offered her whatever she wished. Prompted by her mother, Salome asked for the head of John the Baptist on a platter. As Augustine said, *"Veritas parit odium"*—"Truth begets hatred." Neither Herod nor Herodias could bear to hear the truth about their relationship.

John's disciples buried his body and then hurried off to tell Jesus. At last John's preaching had hit home to his followers—they went to Jesus.

Various Opinions Concerning Jesus

A couple of weeks after John's death, near the end of March, Herod returned to Tiberias. When he got there, everyone was talking about Jesus. The works of Jesus and the mission of the apostles were having their effect. Some said John had come back to life. Others said He was Elijah. Herod was perplexed. He wanted to see this Jesus, simply to be entertained by Him.

Return of the Apostles

So when the apostles returned from their mission to Capernaum in the early weeks of April, Jesus, to give them a much-needed rest and to avoid meeting Herod, took them across the lake from Capernaum in Peter's boat.

THE DECISIVE TEST FOR MEMBERSHIP IN THE KINGDOM

The Multiplication of the Loaves, April, A.D. 29
(*Jn.* 6:1-15)

The disciples rowed leisurely across the lake in a northeastern direction to the Plain of Bataiha about four miles away.

The crowd, however, followed them by land. By land, the Plain of Bataiha was about five miles from Capernaum, or two hours, by foot. So when Jesus arrived, the crowd was already there—that ended their rest. But with His usual graciousness, Jesus welcomed them and began to teach them until late afternoon.

.Then He asked Philip about buying bread. Philip's hometown was Bethsaida just three miles away. If there were a bakery around, Philip would know. But Philip was confounded; he blurted out that two hundred days' wages would not be enough to get just a little for each. The men alone, not counting the women and the children, numbered five thousand. In fact this was one of the largest crowds that Jesus had yet addressed. They had come from the north of Palestine, from Galilee and the Decapolis.

Andrew, to bail out Philip, mentioned there was a boy with five barley loaves, the food of the poor, and two fish. "But," Andrew went on, "what good are these for so many?" Strange, isn't it, that neither Philip nor Andrew counted on Jesus? Without Jesus, problems remain; with Him, they are solved. He can do so much with so little. They both should have learned that at Cana where He changed water into wine.

So Jesus ordered the disciples to get the people to recline on the grass—grass was a sign of springtime and so Passover time. Reminiscent of the groupings of the Israelites in the desert (*Ex.* 18:21-25), they sat the people in fifty rows with a hundred people in each row. Then Jesus took the loaves and the fish and blessed them, broke them, and gave them to the disciples to distribute to the people. The miracle of multiplication took place in His hands, whereas the distribution was made by the disciples. They came back again and again to Jesus to fill their baskets.

When all had been fed, Jesus told them to gather the leftovers, so that they might value God's gifts, realize the magnitude of the miracle, and learn that in giving one receives.

When the people saw this sign, they were all for making Jesus their king. Nationalistic feelings always ran high at Passover time. After a whole year of teaching, the people still did not understand the nature of the kingdom He had come to found.

When it was evening, the disciples embarked in a boat and headed for Bethsaida. They hugged the coastline, intending to pick up Jesus after His dismissing the crowd. Jesus Himself fled to the mountain on the east side of the plain to be alone in order to pray. Twice Jesus prayed all night: once, before choosing the Twelve; and here, before promising the Eucharist, which He was going to do on the following Sabbath in Capernaum.

Jesus Walks on Water (*Jn.* 6:16-21)

While Jesus was at prayer, a strong wind arose, churning up the lake. The apostles decided to wait no longer for Jesus and headed for Capernaum. The storm winds increased in fury and drove them off their course. They were making little headway. Jesus, always so concerned about His own, was aware of their plight and at three o'clock in the morning, He came to them walking on the water. Seeing Him, they began to be afraid. Quickly, Jesus hastened to reassure them, "It is I. Do not be afraid." Their fear left them, for instantly the boat landed on the Plain at Genesareth, just about four miles south of Capernaum.

There they had breakfast from the leftovers of the miracle the day before. Then they slowly wended their way to Capernaum. Late in the afternoon, the crowds from the other side of the lake also arrived. Jesus spoke to them of bread; fourteen times He mentioned the word "bread." Since it was late Friday night, Jesus concluded His talk with the intention of developing it further the next day, the Sabbath, in the synagogue of Capernaum.

The Discourse on the Bread of Life (*Jn.* 6:25-59)

On the next day, the Sabbath, Jesus spoke about three kinds of bread.

The past bread: the manna (*Jn.* 6:26-34) which Moses had brought down from Heaven to nourish the life of the body. Jesus had hoped that His feeding Israel in the desert two days before would convince them that here was the prophet like Moses. He hoped they would begin to believe in Him.

The present bread: the teaching of the Word made flesh, the bread of the Word meant to nourish the life of faith within the people (*Jn.* 6:35-47).

The future bread: not His words, but the Word Himself made flesh, to be eaten like the manna to nourish the life of love within God's people (*Jn.* 6:48-59)—the Most Holy Eucharist!

The Holy Eucharist, the Decisive Test of Faith (*Jn.* 6:60-72)

At Nazareth His own had rejected Him. Now, when He promised to give His flesh to eat, His adopted city rejected Him—"This saying is hard; who can accept it? They no longer accompanied Him."

Jesus turned to the Twelve and asked them, "Do you also want to leave?" The Eucharist was the test. Peter gloriously passed it, as did all the rest, save Judas.

The promise of the Eucharist was made in the context of

two miracles: the multiplication of the loaves and the walking on water. The miracle of the loaves showed that Jesus could do anything He wanted with bread; the walking on the water showed that His body could defy the laws of nature. Jesus said the Eucharist requires faith. These two miracles should have evoked faith. But for the people, it did not; only the Twelve, except for Judas, believed.

Jesus had all but bribed the people to accept His words. He had dazzled them with wonders, almost blinded them with miracles, and when He had clearly shown He was more than man, He fired their imaginations with a breathtaking promise: everlasting life without hunger or thirst. What more could he offer? What else would entice? Were these not enough to give them the will to believe? And yet they would not!

Peter alone speaking for the apostles confessed, "We have come to believe and are convinced that you are the Holy One of God."

Note
Herod the Great (37-4 B.C.)

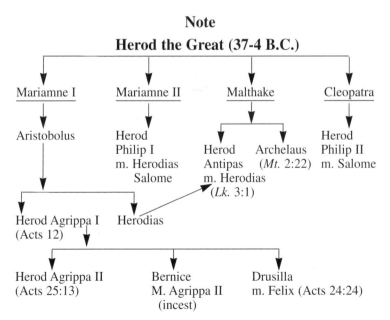

Chapter 7

Jesus Promises a Head for the Kingdom, One to Take His Place

THE SECOND PASSOVER, MONDAY, APRIL 18, A.D. 29

There has always been a question of whether the public ministry of Jesus was two or three years. John's Gospel mentions three Passover feasts, implying a ministry of two full years. The second Passover is mentioned in *John* 6:4. It is identified with the unnamed feast of *John* 5:1.

Many noted Scripture scholars think Chapter 5 of John's Gospel is out of place, that it should follow Chapter 6, not precede it. Such a transposition is not arbitrary, but thoroughly warranted by the total lack of coherence of Chapters 5 and 6 as they now stand. If you transpose them, so that Chapter 5 would follow Chapter 6, then everything falls into place. The sequence of events follows in orderly fashion.

In any case, the tradition of a two-year ministry goes back to the early Church. Writers like St. Irenaeus, St. Epiphanius, St. Cyril of Alexandria favored it. So do we. In that case, the ministry of Jesus would extend from His baptism in January, A.D. 28 to His death at the Passover of A.D. 30.

THE CURE AT THE POOL OF BETHESDA (*Jn.* 5:1-15)

Jesus, like every God-fearing Jew, went up to Jerusalem to celebrate the Feast of the Passover. Just north of the

Temple, near the present Church of St. Anne, there was a pool named Bethesda. From present excavations, we know that it was rectangular in shape and about 350 feet long and 200 feet wide and 25 feet deep, surrounded on all four sides by porches. Across the middle ran a fifth porch, dividing the pool into two sections.

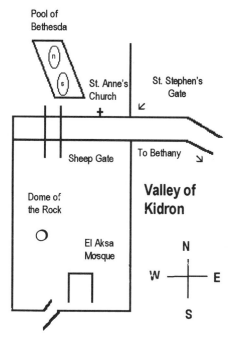

Pool of Bethesda

St. Anne's Church

St. Stephen's Gate

Sheep Gate

To Bethany

Dome of the Rock

Valley of Kidron

El Aksa Mosque

N

W — E

S

According to the historian Eusebius, one of these pools was used for washing sheep before sacrificing them in the temple. It was near the Sheep Gate leading into the temple. The pool was fed by a subterranean spring, which bubbled up intermittently. Its waters were supposed to have curative powers at the time of the bubbling. Thus in the porches lay multitudes of the sick, the lame, the blind, the paralyzed, waiting for the stirring of the waters.

One day during the feast, Jesus came to this assemblage of miseries. He picked out only one person, a man who had been paralyzed 38 years. Jesus asked him if he wanted to get well. The cripple said yes, he wanted to be cured, but he had no one to put him into the water when it bubbled up. Jesus said, "Rise, take up your mat and walk." The man did. He arose, took up his mat and walked away. But it happened to be the Sabbath; so when the Jews saw him carrying his mat, they indignantly pointed out to the man that he could not carry a mat on the Sabbath. The man retorted, "He who cured me told me to carry it." "Who is the man?" they asked. The man did not know, for Jesus had slipped away to avoid the crowd gathering because of the miracle.

Later, the cured man went to the Temple to give thanks to God. There, Jesus met him and warned him to sin no more lest something worse happen to him. What could be worse than 38 years of paralysis? Surely, we have a hint here of hell.

The man, perhaps thinking to extol Jesus, returned to the Jews and told them that it was Jesus who had cured him. Instead of rejoicing with the man and being grateful to Jesus, these envious and malicious men challenged Jesus.

JESUS CLAIMS DIVINITY (*Jn.* 5:19-30)

They attacked Him not only for telling the man to carry a mat on the Sabbath, but for working miracles on the Sabbath. Jesus, trying to help them, responded that God works on the Sabbath in preserving creation, so does the Son. God gives life, so does the Son. God does not judge, as you are misjudging me; He has given judgment over to the Son. These Jews were no fools; they were among the most learned men in the nation, so they didn't miss the point Jesus was making. Rightly, they concluded that Jesus was making Himself equal to God.

JESUS BACKS UP HIS CLAIM TO DIVINITY (*Jn.* 5:31-47)

Jesus was so fearless and still so kind. Patiently, He tried to make them see how right He was by citing four witnesses: first, John the Baptist; secondly, His works; then His Father's voice; and finally the Scriptures. But it was all to no avail. There are none so blind as those who will not see.

They would not be content with anything but His death. So Jesus left Judea and headed for Galilee to return to His headquarters in Capernaum (*Jn.* 7:1).

JESUS AND THE PHARISEES, CAPERNAUM, MAY A.D. 29 (*Mk.* 7:1-23)

Jesus, perhaps, hoped that in Galilee, He would be beyond the reach of the Pharisees of Jerusalem. But it was not to be, for these hellish fiends dogged His steps, and did everything they could to find something to discredit Him in the eyes of the people. An opportunity presented itself when Jesus and His disciples were at a meal in the house of a friendly Pharisee in Capernaum. They had not washed their hands before eating. So His enemies asked, "Why do your disciples not follow the tradition of the elders and eat with unclean hands?"

The Mosaic law made no mention of washing before meals. This was a Pharisaic invention, regarded more important than the law itself. There were over six hundred such prescriptions. Some even nullified the Law of God. For instance, the Pharisees allowed a son, bound by the fourth commandment to help needy parents, to escape this obligation by vowing his money to God. This he did simply by saying, *"Corban."* It was a fictitious consecration, enabling one to use one's money without giving it to anyone else.

The upshot of all these traditions of the elders was to reduce the Jewish religion to legalism in the worst sense of

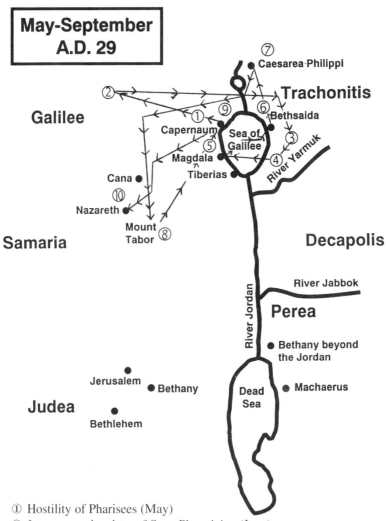

① Hostility of Pharisees (May)
② Jesus cures daughter of Syro-Phoenician (June)
③ Jesus cures deaf-mute (July)
④ Second multiplication of loaves and fish
⑤ Hostility of Pharisees
⑥ Jesus cures a blind man
⑦ Confession of Peter
⑧ Transfiguration (August)
⑨ Temple tax and teaching
⑩ Nazareth (September)

the term. Emphasis was put on externals, on observing man-made traditions. The soul, and the practice of virtue, was entirely forgotten. Thus the prophet Isaiah could say, "This people honors me with their lips, but their hearts are far from me."

THE SYCRO-PHOENICIAN WOMAN, JUNE, A.D. 29 (*Mt.* 15:21-28)

Jesus had had it with them, so He left Capernaum. He would return there only once more. For all practical purposes, He was finished with the people of the lakeside. For the first time in His public ministry Jesus left the promised land. Where He went does not matter. He headed toward the coastal region of Tyre and Sidon. Though the attitude of the people and the hostility of the Pharisees and Herod Antipas played a part in His going out of the Holy Land, yet the main reason for this journey was to be alone with His apostles, to complete their training and to prepare them to make an act of faith in His divinity.

His fame had reached even these parts. A Syro-phoenician woman (Justa), with a faith as strong as that of the centurion, begged Jesus to drive the demon out of her daughter (Bernice). Not wanting to attract a crowd, Jesus ignored her and entered the home of a friendly Jew to dine. But she would not be put off; she burst into the house and fervently pleaded once again with Jesus for her daughter.

Jesus was touched by the tenacity of the woman. He liked her and began to parry words with her. He told her in a kindly manner that His favors were restricted to the children of the household (the Jews); the Gentiles (the dogs) must wait till their time comes. The woman saw that she was disarming Jesus, so she wittily retorted that even dogs are part of the household and therefore do not have to wait; they were entitled to eat the scraps that fall from the table of their masters. Jesus marveled at her faith and told her to return home for the demon had gone out of her daughter. She believed; and, when she reached home, she found the child lying in bed with the demon gone. From this incident, Jesus hoped that the apostles would see that the Gentiles were not beyond the pale of salvation.

JESUS HEALS A DEAF-MUTE, JULY, A.D. 19 (*Mk.* 7:31-37)

Jesus and His apostles kept on the march, avoiding crowds. As they walked, Jesus taught them. They went north toward Sidon, then southeast to the Jordan River, probably crossing it at a bridge about ten miles north of where the Jordan enters the Sea of Galilee. They continued southward to the region called Decapolis—a federation of ten cities with a predominantly Greek population.

In this region Jesus cured a man who had been deaf and dumb. Jesus took him apart from the crowd to save him any embarrassment. Using sign language, Jesus stirred up his faith and communicated to him what He was about to do.

The gestures Jesus used here must have profoundly touched the apostles, for they are still used in the administration of the Sacrament of Baptism. [2]

THE SECOND MULTIPLICATION OF THE LOAVES, JULY A.D. 29 (*Mk.* 8:1-10)

The Jews of the district followed Jesus; they were reluctant to let Him go. To Jesus, these Jews living outside Palestine were the lost sheep of Israel, so He instructed them.

More than 4,000 of them followed Him down to the edge

---

2. Right after infant Baptism, four ceremonies follow: the anointing with chrism, the clothing with the white garment, the lighted candle, and the Ephphetha, or Prayer over ears and mouth.

While touching ears and mouth, the celebrant says: "The Lord Jesus made the deaf hear and the dumb speak. May He soon touch your ears to receive His word, and your-mouth to proclaim His faith, to the praise and glory of God the Father. Amen.

of the lake. Almost in the same spot where, about four months before, He had fed 5,000, He repeated the same miracle and fed 4,000 with seven loaves and a few fish. We can well imagine the impact this great miracle had on the minds and hearts of the apostles.

Then Jesus dismissed the well-fed crowd and got into a boat. It was probably Peter's boat fetched from Bethsaida, his home port. They crossed the lake, sailed past Capernaum, and headed farther south, landing late in the evening somewhere along the southern end of the Plain of Gennesareth near Magdala.

The next morning, the enemies of Jesus—their spies kept them well informed as to His whereabouts—came from Magdala and began disputing with Him about His Messianic claims. Pretending good will, they asked for a sign from Heaven. Jesus saw their hypocrisy; and He sighed from the depths of His spirit and said, *"Why does this generation seek a sign?"* (*Mk.* 8:12). Sadly, He appealed to them, saying, *"You can read the signs in the sky and predict the weather; why then can you not read the heavenly signs worked by me?"*

One gets the feeling that Jesus had almost given up on them, for He left them, got into the boat again, and sailed for Bethsaida.

On the way He was sad and deep in thought: sad at the hardness of heart of His enemies and deep in thought about the effect their opposition might have on His apostles. At midday, when the question of bread arose, Jesus got His chance to say something. "Beware of the leaven of the Pharisees and Sadducees." Then they understood He was telling them to beware of the teaching of the Pharisees and the Sadducees that corrupts like leaven (*Mt.* 16:12).

A BLIND MAN AT BETHSAIDA, JULY, A.D. 29
(*Mk.* 8:22-26)

They docked at Bethsaida late in the afternoon. There, a blind man was brought to Him. The people entreated Jesus to touch him. To avoid any show, Jesus led the man outside the village. He did not cure the blind man instantly, but gradually—the only gradual cure in the Gospels.

This was the last lesson Jesus wished to give the apostles before the confession of Peter. He was teaching them that their realization of Him as Messiah was also a gradual thing. All the miracles they had witnessed were meant to open their eyes little by little so that at Caesarea-Philippi the full light of faith would dawn on them, and they would see Jesus for who He really was.

THE CONFESSION OF PETER: PROMISE OF PRIMACY, JULY, A.D. 29 (*Mt.* 16:13-20)

From Bethsaida Jesus led His apostles north to Caesarea-Philippi, 29 miles away. The tetrarch Philip had rebuilt the city Paneas and renamed it Caesarea in honor of Augustus. It was called Caesarea-Philippi to distinguish it from Caesarea on the Mediterranean.

Here, in this region bordering the Holy Land, Jesus gave His apostles their final test. They had been with Him eighteen months. They had witnessed His miracles and heard His words. Had their eyes been opened? Did they see? Hopefully, He asked the crucial question: "Who am I to you?"

Peter rose to the occasion and confessed that Jesus was the Messiah, the true Son of God. Jesus was elated! His teaching and preaching and miracles had taken hold. His training had succeeded. There was joy in His voice as He unfolded the part to be played by Peter in the kingdom, which He now called "church" for the first time.

He promised to make Peter the head of His Church, the rock, against which the gates of the netherworld shall not prevail. Unity was to be the hallmark of His Church, and Peter and his successors were to secure this unity.

Then by the metaphor of the keys, He showed that Peter would be the "key man" in His Church, His vicar on earth, the one to take His place, the one to wield absolute and universal power (*Is.* 22:22). "Who hears you hears me."

And since the kingdom on earth is a preparation for the kingdom of Heaven, all that he and his successors will do on earth will be ratified in Heaven. With this great promise, Jesus brought to an end the first stage of His mission, the founding of His Kingdom, the Church.

The objective of Jesus' life on earth was twofold: (1) to redeem the world by His passion, death and resurrection; and (2) to found a Church to bring His redemption to all mankind—all times and places.

Having finished His second objective, Jesus now turned the attention of His apostles to His first objective: the redemption of mankind by His death and resurrection. Up to this point, He had led them northward to Caesarea-Philippi to Peter's confession; now He changed direction and started to lead them southward to Jerusalem where He was going to die.

PART II

THE REDEMPTION

Chapter 8

Winding Down the Galilean Ministry

THE TRANSFIGURATION, AUGUST 6, A.D. 29
(*Mt.* 17:1-8; *Lk.* 9:28-36)

After six days, Jesus came to Mt. Tabor, in southeastern lower Galilee. (Some propose that the mountain of the transfiguration is Mt. Hermon, near Caesarea-Philippi.) We opt for Mt. Tabor, which rises 1650 feet out of the Plain of Esdraelon like a camel's hump.

There is a special reason for linking this scene with Peter's confession of faith and with Jesus' prediction of His passion and death. At the transfiguration, Jesus let the sun of His divinity shine through the cloud of His humanity. This shining moment of glory, plus the voice from the cloud, affirmed Peter's confession at Caesarea-Philippi that Jesus is truly the Son of God.

Moses and Elijah, representatives of the law and the prophets, appeared, making it clear that the teachings of Jesus not only were not opposed to the Old Testament, as the Pharisees had charged, but that He was the One of whom the law and the prophets spoke. And they both spoke about the very thing Jesus had predicted, namely His death. Then the voice from the cloud went on to say, for Peter's benefit, "Listen to Him"—even when He talks about death and resurrection!

This extraordinary scene was meant to help the apostles over the scandal of the cross.

THE COMING OF ELIJAH (*Mt.* 17:9-13)

The appearance of Elijah at the transfiguration—rather a bit late in our Lord's life—caused the apostles to ask Jesus, "Why do the scribes say that Elijah must come first before the Messiah?"

Graciously, as always, Jesus, as they came down the mount, explained that the Elijah to come before the Messiah was not the prophet himself, but one like the prophet, having his zeal and fearlessness. This one was John the Baptist. As Elijah suffered from a wicked King Ahab and an evil woman, Jezebel (1 *Kings* 19), so John also suffered at the hands of a wicked King Herod and an evil woman, Herodias.

A POSSESSED BOY (*Mk.* 9:13-28)

When Jesus came down from the mount of transfiguration, a great crowd met Him. Something of the mountain glory must have still lingered on His face, for on seeing Jesus, the crowd was utterly amazed and struck with fear.

His coming was most opportune, for His disciples, who in the past had cast out devils, were unable to do so for the possessed boy here. The local Jewish leaders didn't make matters any easier with their cynical comments. The failure of the apostles had also shaken the boy's father's faith. Jesus quickly sized up the situation. The crowd that had gathered around hoped to see a spectacle. To them Jesus said, "O faithless generation."

His immediate concern was to build up the father's faith. The boy's father said to Jesus, "If you can do anything, . . . help us." Jesus could hardly believe His ears. "If you can?" He asked. "Don't you realize," He said, "that everything is possible to one who has faith?" The boy's father understood, for he cried out, "I do believe, help my unbelief!" Jesus cured the boy because of his father's faith.

Privately, Jesus explained to the apostles why they had

been unsuccessful in curing the lad: lack of faith on the part of the people, and lack of prayer on their part.

Probably on this occasion, when alone with the apostles, Jesus might have told them about His temptations in the desert after His baptism, and how He had been able to conquer the devil by praying and fasting forty days and nights. He so wanted them to learn that prayer and fasting were the lever and fulcrum needed to oust the devil out of the world.

THE SECOND PREDICTION OF THE PASSION
(*Mk.* 9:29-31)

The voice from Heaven at Jesus' transfiguration had said to Peter, James and John, "Listen to him"; so after leaving that place, as they were passing through Galilee, heading toward Capernaum, Jesus once more confided to His apostles saying, *"The Son of Man is to be handed over to men and they will kill him, and three days after his death he will rise."* The thought of His coming death weighed heavy on His mind. But Jesus got small consolation from the apostles. They did not understand the saying, and they were afraid to question Him.

THE TEMPLE TAX, SEPTEMBER, A.D. 29
(*Mt.* 17:23-26)

Three months had passed since Jesus and His apostles had gone from Capernaum. On His return there, the collectors of the temple tax, never giving Jesus the benefit of the doubt, insinuated to Peter that Jesus had kept away from the town for three months just to avoid paying the tax.

Before the destruction of the Jerusalem temple in A.D. 70, every male Jew over nineteen was obliged to contribute one drachmas annually for the upkeep of the temple. This tax was collected during the time between the feast of Passover and the feast of Tabernacles, now just a few weeks away.

So the tax collectors asked Peter, "Doesn't your Master

pay the temple tax?" With his usual impetuosity, Peter answered, "Of course He does"; and he hurried home to get the money. Jesus was already there. Before Peter could speak, Jesus asked him, "From whom do kings receive tribute—from their sons or from others?" Peter answered, "From others." And Jesus said, "The sons are exempt."

What Jesus meant was clear. He is the Son of God and so not subject to a tax for His Heavenly Father's house here on earth. But for the sake of peace, Jesus had Peter catch a fish; in its mouth he found a stater, about 64 cents, enough to pay the tax for Himself and Peter.

JESUS TEACHING THE TWELVE, SEPTEMBER, A.D. 29

On Humility (*Mt.* 18:1-5)

Before this temple tax incident and while the apostles had been on the road to Capernaum, the disciples were discussing the kingdom of Jesus; they were disputing as to who should be the greatest in the kingdom. Each felt sure of his own ability.

Jesus knew their thoughts. So when He was all alone with them in Peter's house at Capernaum, skilled teacher that He was, Jesus looked about for some illustration to impress upon the Twelve that true greatness lay in self-conquest. He found His visual aid in a small boy.

Each of the apostles believed the kingdom of Jesus would be like that of Herod and the Romans: made up of rulers and subjects. Jesus pointed out that the relationship in His kingdom would be more like that between a father and his son, that His kingdom is a family, not a military organization. What He was looking for in the members of His kingdom was a childlike simplicity, trust, and confidence, like that of St. Therese, the Little Flower of Jesus.

On Tolerance (*Mk.* 9:37-39)

Jesus' teaching bothered John, for this son of thunder a short while back had dealt harshly with another: he had forbidden one who was not a follower of Jesus to cast out devils. Now he wondered if he had done the right thing. Jesus said, "Do not prevent him. . . . For whoever is not against us is for us." Little by little Jesus was teaching them tolerance.

On Charity (*Mt.* 10:41-42)

Then in His easy manner, Jesus returned to the image of a child. This time He wished to emphasize the dignity, not the humility, of a disciple. As the father loves his child, so Jesus loves His disciples. So close is He to them and they to Him that what is done to them, He considers as done to Himself. Hence a cup of cold water given them for His sake would be rewarded.

On Avoiding Scandal (*Mt.* 18:6-14)

Continuing with the image of a child, Jesus spoke of scandalizing little ones. "Whoever causes one of these little ones to sin, it would be better for him to have a great millstone hung around his neck and to be drowned in the depths of the sea." And the reason He gave for this was that their angels in Heaven always look upon the face of My Heavenly Father.

In fact, so precious is the human soul in the eyes of the Father that should one be lost, then, like good shepherds, they must leave the ninety-nine to find it. Jesus was driving home to His apostles that the salvation of souls is the highest law, urging them on to the greatest zeal.

On Fraternal Correction (*Mt.* 18:15-18, 21-35)

Not only are they to search out the lost; but they are to teach and exercise the greatest of patience. Even if someone sins again and again, and repents, they are to forgive him. Jesus did away with all counting and bookkeeping. If a person is sorry, forgive him no matter how many times he offends—even seventy times seven times.

Jesus then made it clear why this ought to be by the parable of the unforgiving servant. By sin we contract an infinite debt with God; yet when a person offends us, he contracts only a finite debt. The contrast between the two debts is like a million to one, like the bountiful ocean and a drop of water in the ocean. Since God forgives us the million, the least we can do is to forgive the pittance.

On Avoiding the Occasions of Sin (*Mk.* 9:42-49)

There is a danger, Jesus cautioned; namely, in teaching others, one could be lost. So Jesus warned them not to neglect themselves, for their souls were worth more than the whole world. One way to be on guard is to avoid all the occasions of sin.

On the Power of United Prayer (*Mt.* 18:19-20)

Another way to insure one's salvation is by prayer—united prayer. United prayer is powerful, because Jesus promised that where two or three are gathered in His Name, He would be there. Hence united prayer is all-powerful, for the Father will refuse His Son nothing.

It was now near the end of September; Jesus left Capernaum for Nazareth. No crowds lined the road to bid Him adieu; no regrets were expressed at His departure. On the high cliffs above Magdala, Jesus looked back at the cities where He had worked great miracles and preached for over a year—yet how small was the harvest. As at the end of His Judean ministry, Jesus would weep over Jerusalem, so here Jesus lamented: *"Woe to you, Corozain! Woe to you, Bethsaida! . . . As for you, Capernaum: you will go down to the nether world. On the day of judgment, it will be more tolerable for Sodom"* (*Mt.* 11:20-24).

How sad an ending to His ministry by the Sea of Galilee!

Chapter 9

Feast of Tabernacles, October 15-22, A.D. 29
The Judean Ministry, Oct.-Dec. A.D. 29

JESUS AT NAZARETH (*John* 7:2-13)

Jesus arrived at Nazareth in the autumn time. The harvest was being reaped and people all over the country were preparing to go up to Jerusalem to celebrate the Feast of Tabernacles in thanksgiving for the harvest.

During this feast, people lived in tents (hence the name "tabernacles") in memory of the forty years their ancestors dwelt in tents after leaving Egypt. It was a merry, carnival time, somewhat like our Mardi Gras.

Jesus had small success in Galilee, so His relatives urged Him to go up to Jerusalem during this feast when national spirits ran high, and there proclaim His Messiahship. Jesus refused, probably because such publicity would be dangerous, since the Jews were planning to kill Him (*Jn.* 7:2-13).

Very likely, Jesus left Nazareth the day after the feast had begun; that is, on a Sunday, Oct. 16. Because He wanted to make time, He took the shorter route to Jerusalem by way of Samaria. The Samaritans proved hostile. James and John were for sending down fire from Heaven upon them, just as Elijah had once done (*2 Kgs.* 1:10). But "Jesus turned and rebuked them, and they journeyed to another village" (*Lk.* 9:52-56). Perhaps that other village was Sichar, the home of the Samaritan woman.

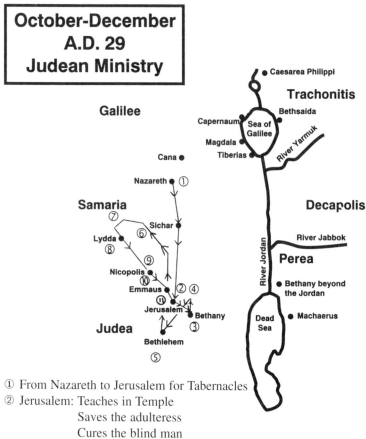

October-December
A.D. 29
Judean Ministry

① From Nazareth to Jerusalem for Tabernacles
② Jerusalem: Teaches in Temple
      Saves the adulteress
      Cures the blind man
③ Bethany: Parable of the Good Shepherd
      Mission of the 72
      Parable of the Good Samaritan
      Mary and Martha
④ Mount of Olives: Teaches *Our Father*
⑤ Bethlehem: Cures the possessed, dines with a Pharisee
      Coastal Region
⑥ Parable of the Rich Fool
⑦ Trust in Providence
⑧ Parable of the Wedding Feast
⑨ Fire and signs
⑩ Stooped woman is cured
⑪ To Jerusalem for the Feast of Dedication

THE FEAST OF TABERNACLES

The Feast of Tabernacles was one of the three greatest feasts of the Jewish religious year (the other two were Passover and Pentecost). In the year A.D. 29, the Feast probably started on October 15. When the Feast was half over, Jesus arrived in Jerusalem, perhaps on a Wednesday, October 19. He went to the temple and began to teach (*Jn.* 7:14-36).

On His previous visits to the temple, there is no mention of His having taught there. At His first visit on the Passover of A.D. 28, He drove the money-changers out of the temple. At His second visit the Sanhedrin interviewed Him privately. But on this occasion, when time was running out, He acted as an authorized teacher. All wondered where He got His learning. Jesus told them His teaching had a divine origin. He proclaimed Himself as the fulfillment of the very symbolism of this Feast. The reaction was varied. The leaders of the Jews tried to kill Him. The people of Jerusalem fell in with their leaders. The pilgrims were divided in their opinion.

The Feast of Tabernacles was the culminating festival of the Jewish ecclesiastical year. It began on the 15th day of the month and was celebrated for seven days. Three solemn ceremonies marked the event.

First, there were the **libations.** Each day, at the morning sacrifice, in solemn procession with music and song, water was brought to the temple in a golden vessel from the pool of Siloam. Amid trumpet blasts and the singing of psalms, the water was poured out as a libation beside the altar and drained off by a sewer into the Kidron valley.

This ceremony commemorated the water springing miraculously from the rock in the desert of Sin at Massah and Meribah at the touch of Moses' rod (*Ex.* 17:6, *Nm.* 20:11).

On the last and greatest day of the Feast, Jesus stood up

and exclaimed that He was the rock from within whom would flow rivers of living water—the Holy Spirit (*Jn.* 7:37-39).

Dissension followed this claim. Some even wanted to arrest Him, but no one laid hands on Him. Jesus withdrew to the Mount of Olives to spend the night (*Jn.* 7:40-53).

The second ceremony observed at this Feast was that families were to dwell in **tents** for the 8 days of the Feast. The word for "tents" is "tabernacle"; hence the name of the Feast. The tents were made from the boughs of trees and were erected on rooftops or in open spaces in the city or outside the city walls. This ceremony commemorated the forty years Israel dwelt in tents in the desert after leaving Egypt. Naturally, a carnival spirit was present at this time. Sometimes liberties were taken, as happened with the woman caught in the act of adultery (*Jn.* 8:1-11).

The third ceremony of the Feast was that of **lights.** Each evening of the Feast, to illuminate the court of the women, two lofty candelabras, 150 feet high, supporting four immense lamps, were lit. These cast light not only in the temple courts, but far and wide over the city. These lights recalled the pillar of fire guiding the Hebrews in their flight from Egypt into the wilderness (*Ex.* 14:29-20).

Pointing to the light, Jesus remarked: *"I am the light of the world. Whoever follows me will not walk in darkness"* (*Jn.* 8:12).

Then to prove that He was the light of the world, Jesus gave the light of sight to a man born blind by having him wash in the pool of Siloam (*Jn.* 9:1-41).

THE PARABLE OF THE GOOD SHEPHERD
(*Jn.* 10:1-18)

After healing the blind man, Jesus returned to Bethany. The Pharisees had excommunicated the healed blind man and had cast him out of the fold of Israel. This mean action prompted Jesus to tell the parable of the Good Shepherd.

The Pharisees were hirelings; they had no concern for the sheep. In contrast, He said, "I am the good shepherd"—good, because He will lay down His life for the sheep and will lead them, like a new Moses, to the promised land of eternal life.

MISSION OF THE SEVENTY-TWO (*Lk.* 10:1-12)

When the feast of Tabernacles ended, Jesus left Jerusalem. In the next two months (November and December), He sought to evangelize Judea. Around this time, three different men came to Him desiring to follow Him. Jesus laid down three conditions for discipleship: the disciple is homeless; gospel-preaching must take precedence over family ties; and lastly, the disciple must never turn back once he has put his hand to the plough.

Probably from here in Bethany, Jesus dispatched seventy-two disciples. As He had used the twelve apostles eight months earlier to preach the gospel in Galilee, so now He sent out a greater number, from 70 to 72, because of the larger territory to be covered and the shortness of time left to Him. They were to spread the Kingdom of God in Judea and Transjordan (Perea) during the weeks from October 22 to December 22.

We don't know exactly when the seventy-two returned, whether all together or group by group. When they did, and told Jesus of their success, "Lord, even the demons are subject to us because of Your name," Jesus replied jubilantly, "Now is the power of the kingdom of Satan broken. . . ."

That was the theme of William Peter Blattey's book *The Exorcist*. The story begins with a priest archaeologist, Fr. Damien Karras, S.J., excavating ruins near ancient Nineveh. In his digging, he uncovers a green stone head of the demon Pazuzu. Blattey was implying that before the advent of Christianity Satan was in control. The psalmist taunted pagans saying, *"All your gods are demons"* (*Ps.* 96:5).

But after Christ founded His Church, Blattey shows that, face to face with the Church, Satan is powerless. Thus he has Fr. Karras called to Washington from his dig. A girl named Regan is possessed by the devil. What happens? Fr. Karras drives out the demon. Blattey's message is, "In the ancient world, Satan was worshipped; in the Christian world, he is exorcised, driven out." It was this Jesus foresaw when He said, "I have observed Satan fall like lightning from the sky." The Church Jesus was founding signaled the beginning of the end of Satan's rule over mankind.

Still in ecstasy, Jesus praised the Father for revealing His ways to little ones. He invited them to come to Himself— for "my yoke is easy and my burden light" (*Mt.* 11:28-30). Then He called them "blessed," for they saw and heard what prophets and kings longed to see and hear, but did not.

THE GOOD SAMARITAN PARABLE (*Lk.* 10:25-37)

Shortly after the return of the seventy-two, while Jesus was in the synagogue at Bethany, a doctor of the Law asked Him, "Teacher, what must I do to inherit eternal life?" As happened so often, Jesus answered the question by asking one: "What is written in the Law? How do you read it?" The lawyer in essence said, "Love God and love your neighbor." Jesus commended him and said, "Do this and you will live." But to justify himself, the lawyer said, "Who is my neighbor?" He believed his neighbor was exactly what the word meant "the one nearest" to himself, namely his fellow countrymen—he wondered if Jesus would agree.

Jesus answered with the parable of the Good Samaritan. The point of the parable was that need takes precedence over race; that one's neighbor is any person in need. The Priest and the Levite, the wounded man's neighbors, were not neighborly; whereas, the Samaritan, an outcast, was. The parable was made most forceful by having a Samaritan, hated by the Jews, the hero of the story.

Often this parable has been allegorized. The man lying by the roadside, robbed of the life of grace and wounded in mind and will by original sin, can stand for the human race—you and me. The priest and the Levite, who were of no help, can signify the sacrifices of the Old Law, which are of no use in the New Covenant. The Good Samaritan can be Jesus, an outcast to some as the Samaritan was to the Jews. He came unto His own and His own received Him not. No matter, divine physician that He is, He came to heal mankind with the oil and wine of the sacraments and to put all in the care of the Church (the inn), and in the care of its head, Peter and his successors (the innkeeper).

Like Jesus, we all need to be good Samaritans—good neighbors.

MARY AND MARTHA (*Lk.* 10:38:42)

After telling the parable, Jesus went to the home of Martha and Mary. Martha was busy preparing dinner for Jesus and His disciples; whereas Mary sat at His feet and listened to Him. Jesus reproved Martha. Why? To teach that when He is present one ought to sit at His feet. The Good Samaritan parable taught that we ought to serve our neighbor; but this incident taught that we ought to let Jesus administer to us. Only when one listens to Jesus can one become a good Samaritan. Busyness must never crowd out His voice.

THE OUR FATHER (*Mt.* 6:9-15; *Lk.* 11:1-40)

Shortly after the Bethany episode, Jesus journeyed to the Mount of Olives, above the garden of Gethsemani, to pray. Prayer must have transfigured Jesus, for seeing its effect on Him, one of His disciples said, "Lord, teach us to pray." He taught them the *"Our Father."*

Confidence is one of the conditions for fruitful prayer, so He taught us that in praying we ought to go to God as to a father. He once said that if earthly fathers *"who are wicked, know how to give good gifts to their children, how much more will your heavenly Father give good things to those who ask him"* (*Mt.* 7:11).

St. John Damascence defined prayer as "a petition of fitting things from God." In the "Our Father," Jesus listed seven petitions: three concern our relation to God, and three concern our relation to others; between these two sets of three is a petition for temporal needs.

Finally, this prayer includes all people, because it uses the words "our" and "us" but not "my" or "me."

The "Our Father" taught the disciples **what** to pray for; then with the story of the importunate friend, Jesus taught them **how** to pray, namely, with **persistence,** as well as with **confidence** (*Lk.* 11:5-8). In the business world, executives are told that "consistent applied action to a predetermined goal is the key to success." The same is true of prayer: to be a powerful weapon, prayer must be offered consistently and insistently.

BLASPHEMY OF THE PHARISEES
(*Lk.* 11:14-23; 12:1)

As Jesus moved away from the neighborhoods of Jerusalem, He came to the desert of Judea near Bethlehem. There, a man possessed by the devil was brought to him. Jesus cured him. No matter, the Pharisees blasphemed Him, charging that he cast out demons by Beelzebub, the prince of demons. The good Jesus could do no more. His enemies were malicious, willfully blind—the unforgivable sin against the Holy Spirit (*Mt.* 12:22-37).

Such viciousness could not go unchallenged. Jesus feared the common people might be led away from the truth. So he appealed to their common sense: Satan would not fight against himself—a house divided against itself cannot stand. His war was against a foe, not a friend. The conflict was between two kingdoms: God's and Satan's. Neutrality was out of the question. "He who is not with me is against me, and he who does not gather with me scatters."

Concerned lest the crowds be duped or let down their guard, Jesus warned them that Satan is a relentless enemy who never gives up. Nature abhors a vacuum, so does the devil. If a soul is spiritually empty, the devil, even though once driven out, will return with reinforcements and move in and dwell there, so that "the last condition of that person is worse than the first" (*Lk.* 11:24-26).

A woman in the crowd, maybe a servant of Martha, cried out, *"Blessed is the womb that carried you and the breasts at which you nursed"* (*Lk.* 11:27-28). Jesus corrected her and said there is a bond stronger then blood relationship. His mother, though blessed among women as mother, was even more blessed, because she heard the word of God and kept it. She conceived the Word of God first in her heart, then in her womb.

APPEAL FOR A SIGN (*Mt.* 12:38-42)

Having silenced the more hostile wing of the Pharisees, the less rabid element began to question Jesus. They wanted a sign. Jesus refused—a sign was not what was needed, but good will. In cryptic language Jesus hinted at the greatest of all signs—His resurrection.

Using the illustration of a lamp, Jesus showed the Pharisees why a sign would be of no use. They needed more than eyeglasses; they needed eyes (*Lk.* 11:33-36).

DENUNCIATION OF THE PHARISEES, NOVEMBER A.D. 29 (*Lk.* 11:37-52).

One of the Pharisees, perhaps touched by Jesus' brilliant replies to his colleagues, invited Him to dinner. On four occasions in the Gospels, our Lord accepted an invitation to dine at the house of a Pharisee: at Magdala, at Capernaum, this one in Judea (possibly Bethlehem), and the fourth in Perea.

At this particular dinner, St. Luke has Jesus denouncing the Pharisees by six woes: three against the Pharisees, who had reduced religion to mere externalism, observing the law of Moses; and three against the lawyers, who interpreted the law to suit their fancy.

It is unlikely that Jesus would break out in such condemnation at the table of his host at Bethlehem. Luke is probably summarizing what our Lord said at different times during the Judean ministry. Here at the Pharisee's house was probably where Jesus acknowledged that He could no longer deal gently with the lawyers and Pharisees. St. Matthew puts these woes on the Tuesday of Holy Week (see p. 128).

As dogs race after moving cars, so the Pharisees pressed hard after Jesus and sought to provoke Him on many things, setting traps for Him and plotting to get Him to say something that might incriminate Himself. They seemed incorrigible. Gentleness and humility had not won them over, so Jesus began to speak like the Baptist and utter woes to this brood of vipers.

COURAGE IN PERSECUTION (*Lk.* 12:1-9)

As in the Galilean ministry, Jesus left Galilee for Syrophoenicia and the Decapolis to avoid the hostility of the Pharisees and to complete the training of His apostles, so now here in the Judean ministry, Jesus gave Jerusalem a wide berth to avoid Pharisaic conflicts and to be able to give final instructions to His disciples.

Heading toward the coastal Plain of Sharon, Jesus often spoke to His disciples at night and in whispers. He made it clear to them that no disciple is greater than his master. He was attacked, so would they be. What they needed was courage and fearlessness. "Do not be afraid of them," He told them. "What I say to you in the darkness, speak in the light; what you hear whispered, proclaim on the housetops.

Your Father knows when a sparrow falls to the ground. You are worth more than many sparrows, so do not be afraid" (*Mt.* 10:27-30).

WARNING AGAINST AVARICE (*Lk.* 12:13-21)

We don't know the exact route that Jesus took at this time. But it would seem, He went to Nicopolis near the coastal Plain of Sharon, where agriculture could make men rich. When a man brought a problem here about his inheritance, Jesus warned the people about avarice. He told the parable of the rich man who planned to build bigger barns to house his great harvest and then take his rest. Jesus called him a fool. The lesson was that anyone else who would lay up treasures only on earth and not in Heaven was also a fool!

In the days long before movies and television, kings used to be entertained by jesters, called fools. One king had acquired a fool of such great wit that the king decided to crown him "King of Fools." A mock ceremony of coronation was held. At it the jester was given a crown and a scepter. At the conferring of the scepter, the king said, "Sir Fool, keep this scepter until you meet a fool greater than yourself."

The years rolled by. Then one day the king became mortally ill. As he lay dying, he asked that his jester be brought to his bedside that he might thank him for the years of merriment he had given him and the court.

When the jester entered the king's bedroom, he doffed his cap and bells. As he drew near the king's bedside, the king said, "Sir Fool, I am going on a long journey. Before I go, I want to thank you for all the joy you had brought to me and my court over the years."

"But you'll return, Sire?" asked the fool.

"No," said the king sadly, "from this journey no man returns."

"Then, Sire, you've made preparations for this journey so that where you are going they will receive you as a king?" Sadly, the king said, "I've made no such preparations."

"Sire," the jester questioned in disbelief, "You are going on a long journey from which you will not return, and you have made no preparations? Sire, when you crowned me King of Fools you gave me this scepter and told me to keep it until I met a fool greater than myself." Weepingly, the jester laid his scepter on the king's bed.

TRUST IN DIVINE PROVIDENCE (*Lk.* 12:22-48)

Afterwards, when alone with His disciples, Jesus elaborated on the parable of the rich fool. He reminded His disciples that they must rely on divine providence, not on riches. Unlike the rich fool in the parable, they must always be on the watch, like men awaiting their master's return for a wedding feast, for death comes like a thief in the night.

Peter spoke up. This is the only time he is mentioned as speaking in the Judean ministry. He wondered if our Lord meant this teaching about preparedness to be for the people or just for themselves, their leaders. Jesus implied that He meant it for His disciples. In a sort of an answer to Peter, He said, "Never you mind only about others; just be certain to take care of yourself."

FURTHER INSTRUCTIONS (*Lk.* 12:49-59)

The teachings Jesus was giving upset all human values. He was burning up the wreckage and confusion brought into religion by the false interpretations of the Pharisees. His mission was to set the world on fire, on fire with divine love. "I have come to set the earth on fire." This could be done only through His baptism of fire—His passion and death. And He desired this baptism—"how I wish it were already blazing!"—to conquer the hate and enmity He saw all around Himself and to establish the reign of love.

But the love He was talking about was not peace at any

price. He saw people all around Him fearing to rock the boat; therefore giving consent to evil by their silence and do-nothing attitude.

Peace with God and peace of conscience are to be devoutly desired. Peace with others, however, must be conditional. It is all right if others do not interfere with one's peace with God and one's peace of conscience; but if they do, if all the attempts at instruction, reconciliation, and harmony have failed, then war against them is in order—"I have come to bring the sword" (*Mt.* 10:34).

Meanwhile, the Pharisees and Sadducees continued to shadow Jesus. With great forbearance, Jesus still retaliated with love. He even tried to share with His enemies what He had said to His disciples about being prepared. Time was running out for them; and they were still warring against the Kingdom of God.

In a desperate effort to get them to change, Jesus said, "When you see clouds from the west, you know that it will rain. When a burning wind from the south blows, you know it will be hot. You know how to forecast the weather from the signs in the sky, why can't you read the signs of my divine message?" He warned them, He urged them, He prodded them, to act now before it was too late.

NECESSITY OF REPENTANCE (*Lk.* 13:1-9)

Jesus was not far from Jerusalem at this time, probably near Emmaus. Knowing He was a Galilean, some friends reported to Him the latest Roman brutality: Pilate killing some Galileans. This could have caused a falling out between Pilate and Herod, for Galilee was under Herod's jurisdiction. Barabbas could have been the leader of this revolt.

The Jews felt that physical calamity was invariably a punishment for moral evil. To correct this error, Jesus recalled another incident of sudden death—when the tower

of Siloam fell, killing 18 men. The Jews felt that these people had been sinners. Jesus said their thinking was wrong.
He asked, "Do you think these eighteen people were more
guilty than all the other dwellers in Jerusalem?" In
Jerusalem many were devoid of good works, like the barren
fig tree. Still, they were not killed. "But beware," Jesus
warned, "Unless you repent and bear fruit, you too will all
perish in the end!"

CURE OF A BENT WOMAN ON THE SABBATH (*Lk.* 13:10-17)

Did His enemies respond? Did the fire Jesus came to light
on earth begin to burn? At this particular time in Judea, it did
not. Very likely, these inveterate enemies of Jesus planted a
stooped woman in the synagogue at Emmaus to see if He
would break the Sabbath and cure her. Jesus did cure her, for
He pitied this woman, who had suffered from a spinal defor-
mity for eighteen years. Instead of rejoicing with Him and
her, they condemned Jesus for healing on the Sabbath. Thus
they merited their own condemnation.

Jesus went from there to Jerusalem for the Feast of the
Dedication.

Chapter 10

Feast of Dedication, December 22, A.D. 29
Perean Ministry: December, A.D. 29—April, A.D. 30

The Feast of the Dedication (in Hebrew, *Hanukkah*) was not one of the three original festivals dating from the time of the Exodus (*Lv.* 23). It was instituted by Judas Maccabeus in 165 B.C. after he had won back the temple profaned by Antiochus Epiphanes. It was also called the Feast of Lights, because the temple was brightly illuminated on the first and last days of the feast. Attendance for the feast was not obligatory, still great crowds came to Jerusalem to celebrate it.

JESUS AND THE FATHER ARE ONE (*John* 10:22-39)

Because it was wintertime, Jesus walked in the covered porches of the temple, Solomon's colonnade. The Jews, the leaders of the people, wanted to know if He was the Messiah. It was an insidious question. Both the Jewish leaders and the Romans looked upon the Messiah as an earthly prince. Should He claim to be the Messiah, the Jewish leaders could have denounced Him to the Romans as a revolutionary. Jesus simply said, "I act like God's Son, why don't you believe me?" Then Jesus explained, "You know why you don't believe? You're not my sheep. For my sheep hear my voice and follow me and I give them life eternal. They shall not perish and no man may snatch them from me. I know this for certain, because I and the Father are one."

That claim—being one with the Father—infuriated the religious leaders. It was clear to them He was making

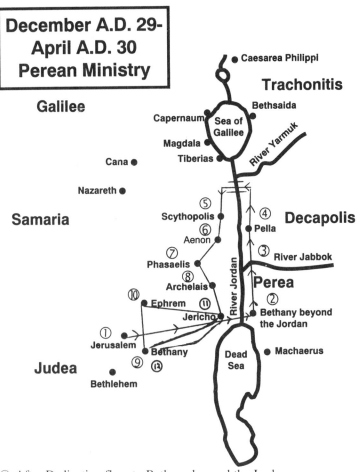

① After Dedication flees to Bethany beyond the Jordan
② Starts Perean ministry
③ Parables: Lost Sheep, Lost Coin, Lost Son
④ Four lessons on riches
⑤ The cure of the ten lepers
⑥ Teachings on prayer
⑦ Teachings on Marriage, Divorce, Celibacy, and the Rich Young Man
⑧ Laborers in Vineyard, news of Lazarus' illness
⑨ Raising of Lazarus
⑩ Goes to Ephrem
⑪ Cures a blind man, dines with Zaccheus
⑫ Anointed at home of Simon

Himself equal to God. To them that was blasphemy. Therefore they picked up rocks to stone Him.

JESUS IN PEREA, JAN.-FEB. A.D. 30

As a result, Jesus fled to Bethany beyond the Jordan. There were two villages called Bethany. One was on the east side of the Mount of Olives, about two miles from Jerusalem, the home of Lazarus and his sisters Mary and Martha, the headquarters of Jesus during His Judean ministry. The other was on the east bank of the Jordan— Bethany beyond the Jordan—the starting-point for the Perean ministry. *"He went back across the Jordan to the place where John first baptized"* (Jn. 10:40).

Perea (Greek for *Transjordan*) was part of the territory of Herod Antipas. It included both the east and the west sides of the Jordan valley. Our Lord's ministry in Perea probably took Him up the east bank and down the west bank of the Jordan river. This, however, is only conjecture.

THE NARROW GATE, JANUARY A.D. 30
(*Lk.* 13:22-30)

In confronting the leaders of the people in Jerusalem, Jesus had said, "I give (my sheep) eternal life, and they shall never perish." As He went through the towns and villages in Perea, someone asked Him if He meant that only a few would be saved. The questioner was of course referring only to his countrymen. (Jews believed all Gentiles would be damned.)

Jesus made two corrections. First, He made it clear that being a Jew is not enough for salvation. Salvation depends, not on race, but on personal holiness. And second, He said that many of the Gentiles will be saved, for some who are last shall be first, and some who are first shall be last.

JESUS AND HEROD (*Lk.* 13:31-33)

On the same day, some Pharisees warned Jesus that

Herod sought His life. Herod was probably at nearby Machaerus at the time. He had killed John; he didn't want to repeat that tragedy. He preferred to scare Jesus away from his territory. Jesus called Herod a fox, cunning and cowardly. Jesus knew he would die only in Jerusalem. He also knew that He had three months more to go. So, despite Herod's threat, He continued His work confidently.

A MAN WITH DROPSY (*Lk.* 14:1-6)

Thus He proceeded northward, up the Jordan valley. He dined on a Sabbath at the home of one of the Pharisees. This was a midday meal. A man, who had dropsy, came to the dining room—again, this may have been another plant to see if Jesus would cure on the Sabbath.

Dropsy was a swelling caused by watery fluid in the body tissues. With His usual concern for people, Jesus cured the man; and, as would be expected, it brought a protest. Jesus answered His protesters, not in anger, but in an effort to win them over by irrefutable logic, saying, *"Who among you, if your . . . ox falls into a cistern, would not immediately pull him out on the sabbath day?"* (*Lk.* 14:5). Simply put, Jesus was asking, can the needs of a dumb animal be given priority over those of a human being?

Even today, we often meet people who are kinder to animals than to human beings. Do we not see bumper stickers that read: "Be a hero save a whale; save a baby, go to jail." True charity makes no distinctions; it is kind to all—to people and beasts alike—but first to people.

THE LAST SEAT (*Lk.* 14:7-14)

Sadly, the people paid no attention to Jesus' logic; they seemed more concerned with getting the seats of honor at the banquet table. At a banquet, couches were arranged in a U-shape. The couch at the curve of the U was the head table.

Watching the guests elbowing their way to the seats of honor, Jesus, not to embarrass them for their breach of etiquette, told the parable of a Wedding Feast. He implied that people ought not to be pushy; rather they ought to appreciate the virtue of humility that puts one high in God's estimation.

Also, noting that His host had invited only the elite to the banquet, Jesus subtly tried to teach him that even the poor, the lame, and the crippled ought to be invited so that he would receive recompense at the resurrection.

PARABLE OF THE GREAT SUPPER (*Lk.* 14:15-24)

Jesus' remark about resurrection caused one of those at table to say, "Blessed is the one who will dine in the kingdom of God." Of course he was thinking that He Himself and his fellow countrymen would be among the diners. With unbelievable patience, Jesus tried to lead them to see that the invitation to the kingdom needed to be responded to. He told a parable of a Great Supper. Those invited spurned the invitation. Either they were too busy or too materialistic or too self-centered.

Likewise, through the prophets, through John the Baptist, and now through Himself, God had been inviting His own people to the kingdom. But because of their greed, pride, ignorance, or sensuality, they were not responding to the Messiah. Should they continue in their obduracy, Jesus warned them gently that they too could be in danger of being left outside and their places taken by the publicans and sinners and Gentiles.

THE COST OF DISCIPLESHIP, FEB., A.D. 30 (*Lk.* 14:25-35)

Jesus then continued to move northward up the eastern bank of the River Jordan. Great crowds followed Him. Their enthusiasm matched that of the Galilean crowds. But like the Galileans, they too hoped for a political Messiah.

Jesus would not encourage these false Messianic hopes.

Instead, as He approached the River Jabbok, a creek that could be forded anywhere, Jesus, ever truthful, (like a Churchill who offered the English, when he became Prime Minister, only blood, sweat, and tears to conquer Hitler) spelled out clearly the cost of discipleship, of following Him.

He urged His disciples to count the cost of discipleship, to take into consideration the strength of resolution needed to make the sacrifices needed to follow Him. With two simple examples, Jesus demonstrated that this was just common sense. If the master of a vineyard planned to build a tower in it, surely he would calculate the cost to see if he had money enough to finish it. In vineyards, towers served as lookouts against thieves, as store rooms, and as lodging for the watchman of the vineyard.

Or if a war threatened to break out at any time, as seemed likely between King Herod and King Aretas, neither king would undertake it if he saw no chance of winning it.

Likewise, whoever wished to be His disciple needed to foresee the sacrifices and self-conquest demanded, else they would become victims to their own weaknesses.

GOD'S MERCY TOWARD SINNERS, FEB. A.D. 30 (*Lk.* 15:1-32)

After Jesus' private chat with His disciples, the Pharisees and the scribes drew near and began to complain, saying, "This man welcomes sinners and eats with them." Jesus countered with three of the most wonderful parables in the whole New Testament, exemplifying God's mercy. To the Pharisees, mercy was weakness; and kindness to sinners unbecoming to a rabbi. To Jesus, God's mercy was above all His works, and so He too would be merciful.

Near the River Jabbok, Jesus explained in the parable of the Lost Sheep that God searches for the sinner much as a shepherd searches for a sheep lost (*Lk.* 15:1-7). In the parable of the Lost Coin, Jesus showed that God is as anxious to find the sinner as a woman is to recover part of her dowry that she had lost (*Lk.* 15:8-10). And in the glorious parable of the Prodigal Son, Jesus said God is like the father waiting for the prodigal to come home (*Lk.* 15:11-32). In this last parable, Jesus also threw in the reaction of the elder brother. He hoped to get the Pharisees to see that their attitude toward sinners was ugly, like that of the elder brother, prompted by an arrogant pride and an unconscionable lack of charity.

The three parables also illustrate that sinners can lose God in one of three ways: by stupidity, like the sheep straying from the flock by nibbling and never looking up; by accident, like the lost coin; or by choice, like the prodigal son. Those lost by stupidity or accident, God seeks; on the contrary, it seems that those lost by willfulness must seek God.

FOUR LESSONS ON WEALTH—PELLA, FEB. A.D. 30 (*Lk.* 16:1-31)

In the parable of the Great Supper, Jesus had barely touched upon the subject of riches. So after the parables on God's mercy toward sinners, Jesus turned His attention to one of the chief causes of sin: the love of money.

At Pella, just north of the River Jabbok, Jesus told the parable of the Unjust Steward (*Lk.* 16:1-12). The lesson Jesus meant to teach was that one ought to be just as prudent in securing eternal salvation as the unjust steward was in securing a comfortable living in this world. Jesus recommended his prudence, but not his dishonesty.

Pursuing the same topic, Jesus pointed out that no man can serve two masters: God and money (*Lk.* 16:13). The Pharisees, who were fond of money, sneered at Him; they were rich and, in their luciferan pride, they believed that they served God.

Again Jesus' reproach was gentle, but firm; He reminded them of what God had said to Samuel, *"Not as man sees does God see, because man sees the appearance but the Lord looks into the heart"* (*1 Samuel* 16:7).

To show that there can be a reversal of roles in the world to come between the haughty rich and the beggarly poor, Jesus told the parable of the Rich Man and Lazarus (*Lk.* 16:19-31).

Near the River Yarmuk, within sight of the Sea of Galilee, where sycamore trees grew with roots in the edge of the water, the apostles, shocked by the dangers of riches, asked Jesus in private to increase their faith. Jesus encouraged them not to fear, for He said: "If you had faith the size of a mustard seed, you would say to this sycamore tree, 'Be uprooted and planted in the sea,' and it would obey you."

Then to make certain that the extraordinary effects of faith, which they would experience in their ministry, might not puff them up with pride, Jesus reminded them that they must think of themselves as servants of God's children and not lord it over them as did the Pharisees (*Lk.* 17:5-10).

At the River Yarmuk, there is a ferry, where Jesus probably crossed the Jordan. Then on the western bank, He began His journey southward toward Jerusalem. Near the city of Scythopolis, on the border between Galilee and Samaria, ten lepers came to Him. They must have known His compassion, for no leper would approach a Rabbi. Nor were they disappointed in their hopes, for Jesus cured the whole lot of them. The ten were one in misery, one in their request, and one in their cure; but they were different in their gratitude. Only one came back to say thanks, and he was a Samaritan (*Lk.* 17:12-19).

Jesus continued southward. It was now February, A.D. 30. He approached Aenon where John the Baptist had preached about the coming of the kingdom of God. But two years had passed, and in their eyes the kingdom had not yet come. So the Pharisees asked Jesus when would the kingdom of God come.

Jesus answered, it would come suddenly, like the lightning in the sky; therefore He warned them to be prepared; not to wallow in a false security as did the people at the time of the Flood in Noah's day, and in the days of Lot, and Sodom and Gomorrah. Like a kind friend, He counseled these His enemies to be prepared, for the judgment would follow this coming—the elect will flock to God, as surely and as swiftly as vultures gather over a corpse.

While still near Aenon, Jesus repeated two teachings on prayer. By the parable of the Unjust Judge (*Lk.* 18:1-8), He taught that one must be persistent in praying—the constancy of the dropping water wears a hole in the rock.

By the parable of the Pharisee and the Publican (*Lk.* 18:9-14), He taught that one must be humble in praying.

The publican stood in the back of the temple; he did not dare to lift his eyes to Heaven; he beat his breast, confessed his sins and asked God, "Be merciful to me the sinner" (that's what he thought he was in comparison with the Pharisee standing up front).

The Pharisee, on the contrary, lifted his head proudly, boasted of his good works, despised others and prayed thus: "I thank you . . . I am not like the rest of men . . . I fast . . . I pay tithes"—I, I, I. St. Augustine asked, "What did he go up to the temple for—to pray, or to praise himself?" Jesus said that the publican went home justified, not the other.

As Jesus proceeded farther south, near Phasaelis, March, A.D. 30, He spoke on marriage, divorce, and celibacy (Mk. 10:2-12).

The Old Law tolerated divorce; the New Law abolished it. In case of adultery, Jesus permitted only separation, but not remarriage. Jesus' reason for this was that God established monogamy at the creation of Adam and Eve. And in expressing married love, two persons become one. "Therefore what God has joined together, no human being must separate." Jesus simply echoed God's law given at the beginning of the race.

It was as though Jesus had said, "Would you take another man's house? If you try to do this, man-made laws would stop you. God's laws are greater than man's. If you take another's wife or husband, then you violate God's law and kill the life of the soul."

When alone with Jesus, the disciples questioned Him that "If this be the case, then it is better not to marry." Their remark about not marrying led Jesus to say a word about the excellence of celibacy. *"There will even be some,"* He said, *"who will voluntarily renounce marriage for the sake of the kingdom of heaven. Whoever can accept this ought to accept it"* (*Mt.* 19:10-12). The Council of Trent (1545-1563) stated that voluntary celibacy practiced from religious motives is more excellent than the married state (Sess. 24, canon 10).

Because He had spoken so beautifully about the holiness of marriage, parents brought their children to Him that He might bless them (*Mk.* 10:13-16).

THE RICH YOUNG MAN (*Mk.* 10:17-31)

As Jesus was leaving Phasaelis, a rich young man came to Him and asked, "Teacher, what good must I do to gain eternal life?" John Paul II begins his great encyclical *Veritatis Splendor* (8/6/93) with this story of the rich young man. Jesus answers the young man's question by telling him that God alone is good. Because He is good, He is most lovable, and so to be loved; and because He is good, He is also the source of morality, of what is good and what is bad. To gain eternal life, therefore, one must love God and keep His commandments. The young man persisted, "I've done this."

There followed the four looks of Jesus. A look of love, when the young man said he had kept all the commandments—"And Jesus, looking upon him loved him." A look of sadness, when the young man refused His invitation to sell all and follow Him. Sadly, Jesus said to His disciples, "It is easier for a camel to pass through the eye of a needle, than for a rich man to enter the kingdom of God." So Jesus looked upon His disciples with a look of encouragement and said nothing is impossible with God. Finally, a look of joy beamed on the face of Jesus when Peter blurted out, "We have given up everything and followed you."

Peter had said, "We've left all and followed thee." It is not enough to just leave all. Plato and Aristotle left all, not to follow Christ, but to follow knowledge. Alexander the Great left all, but to conquer the world. In vain is it to leave all if it is not to follow Christ. The following of Christ is the key to glory and everlasting life. So Jesus said, *"Many that are first will be last, and the last first."* As always, Jesus illustrated what He meant by the parable of the Laborers in the Vineyard (*Mt.* 20:1-16), which concludes with the same phrase: the last shall be first, the first last.

THE PARABLE OF THE LABORERS IN THE VINEYARD, ARCHELAIS, MARCH, A.D. 30

As Jesus proceeded southward from Phasaelis to Archelais, 30 miles northeast of Jerusalem, He passed by the many vineyards of the Jordan Valley. It was springtime, and so a time of feverish activity from daylight to dusk in the vineyards. Since the work was seasonal, it was done by casual labor. Foremen were busy hiring laborers. The Mosaic Law required that wages be paid at the end of each day (*Dt.* 24:15).

Jesus always drank in the beautiful sights of skies and fields. How He loved the outdoors! As He walked, the vineyards He saw probably inspired the striking parable of the

Laborers in the Vineyard.

First of all, Jesus wanted the people to see from the para-ble the graciousness of God His Father, who gives as freely to the last as to the first.

Also, He wished to banish any misgivings that the apos-tles might have had, because they were only poor fisher-men, about their place in His kingdom. All that counted, He told them, was that they labor faithfully in His vineyard. As a note of warning, He hinted that some called first, like Judas and Israel, could fall away; whereas some called last, like Matthias and the Gentiles, could end up first in the kingdom.

THE RAISING OF LAZARUS (*Jn.* 11:1-44)

While at Archelais, a few miles north of Jericho, Mary and Martha sent word to Jesus saying, "Master, the one you love is ill." Some of the greatest prayers in the New Testament are one-liners: "They have no wine"; "Lord, if you will, you can make me clean"; "Remember me when you come into your kingdom."

In their prayer, Mary and Martha mentioned no name; they simply said "the one you love . . . ," in order to protect Jesus whose life was in danger. Still, in their extremity, they knew to whom they could turn for help. While the courier was on his way, Lazarus died.

How the heart of Jesus must have burned with the desire to rush to the aid of those He so fiercely loved. But tough love is sacrificial love. He denied the tug of His heart to win greater blessings for those He loved. His absence from Lazarus' funeral might have occasioned His enemies to sneer and slander Him as an imposter, but that same absence offered Mary and Martha the opportunity to deepen their faith in Him. When at last He did come, Lazarus had already been dead for four days.

Martha ran out to the outskirts of Bethany to meet Him.

She cried out, "Lord, if you had been here, my brother would not have died." How many times during Lazarus' illness she and Mary must have repeated those words. "If only He were here . . ." Now that He was here, Jesus told Martha to have faith. She confessed her faith and raced back to get Mary.

When Mary came to Jesus, she repeated the same words as Martha, "Lord, if you had been here . . ." Mary wept. To the practical Martha, Jesus talked of having faith; but to the emotional Mary, Jesus simply wept with her and asked to be taken to the grave of Lazarus.

At the grave Jesus said, "Take away the stone." When they had, He raised His eyes and prayed to His Father. Then He cried out in a loud voice, "Lazarus, come out!" The dead man came out.

The raising of Lazarus from the dead was the most important miracle of Jesus prior to His own resurrection. It manifested His supreme power over life, since the body of Lazarus had already begun to decompose. Both friends and foes witnessed it, since Bethany was only two miles from Jerusalem.

Some of those who had witnessed the miracle believed. But the Sanhedrin, the highest assembly of government in Israel in the time of our Lord, did not. Caiaphas, the high priest from A.D. 18 to 36, said that "one man should die . . . so that the whole nation may not perish." For he reasoned that if the people accepted Jesus as the Messiah, they would revolt against Rome and Rome would destroy the nation. *"So from that day on they planned to kill him"* (*Jn.* 11:53). Envy, fear, and pride can make us all so blind.

Nicodemus probably tipped Jesus off about the conspiracy, so Jesus withdrew to Ephrem about 17 miles northeast of Jerusalem. Being 2600 feet above sea level, Ephrem overlooked the Judean desert and the Jordan Valley (*Jn.* 11:54-56).

LAST JOURNEY AROUND JERUSALEM

Jesus stayed at Ephrem for a short while. As the Passover feast drew near, He left Ephrem and headed for Jericho. On the way He foretold for a third time, more clearly than ever before, His imminent passion, death, and resurrection (*Mk.* 10:32-45).

Two distinct groups were now with Jesus: the twelve apostles and the other disciples, including women who attended to the material needs of Jesus and His companions.

When Salome, the mother of James and John, heard Jesus' words about His coming death and resurrection, and noting His noble bearing leading His followers like a conqueror into battle, she wanted her sons of thunder to be at His side. So she asked for an honorable place for James and John. Jesus explained that the way to become close to Himself was through suffering.

Her two sons did drink the chalice of the Lord. James was martyred by Herod Antipas in A.D. 44. And John was immersed in a caldron of boiling oil under the Emperor Domitian (A.D. 81-96); but he came out unscathed and was exiled to the Isle of Patmos.

THE BLIND MEN AT JERICHO (*Mk.* 10:46-52)

Jesus was going to Jerusalem to die. He tried to tell the apostles this. But apparently He couldn't get through to them. They too were blind, but mentally. As He was entering Jericho, He cured two blind men, as if to teach His apostles that their eyes would also be opened soon by His death in Jerusalem.

One of the two blind men was named Bartimeus. One lesson he teaches us is to seize the opportunities of grace. Augustine said, "I do not fear the passing by of Jesus, but only that He may never pass by this way again." Had Bartimeus not seized the opportunity present when Jesus passed through Jericho, he would have died a blind man, for this was in fact the last time Jesus ever passed through Jericho—He never came that way again. Hence the Latin adage: *"Carpe diem*—"Seize the opportunity."

JESUS AND ZACCHAEUS (*Lk.* 19:1-28)

In Jericho Jesus dined in the home of Zacchaeus and converted him. At dinner Jesus told the parable of the Gold Coins to alert His followers to trade as Zacchaeus had, to use their graces and not to sit around in idleness.

From Jericho Jesus went on to Bethany. There, he stayed two nights at the home of Mary and Martha. On the second night, Saturday, April 1, A.D. 30, He dined at the home of Simon the Leper in Bethany. Simon was probably indebted to Jesus for having previously cured him of his leprosy (not recorded in the Gospels).

There, Mary anointed His feet with precious ointment; then breaking the jar, she poured the remainder on His head (*Jn.* 12:1-11). The ointment was probably left over from the funeral rites of Lazarus. Mary alone of all those present understood that Jesus was soon to die. Her anointing was a sorrowful farewell.

Chapter 11

Final Ministry in Jerusalem (Holy Week)

JESUS' ENTRY INTO JERUSALEM (PALM SUNDAY), APRIL 2, A.D. 30

Today whenever the Pope appears in procession, the Italians shout, *"Viva il Papa!"* When Jesus entered Jerusalem on the Sunday just before the Passover, the crowd that was with Him when He raised Lazarus from the dead greeted Him with the shout of *"Hosanna!"* an exclamation of joy taken from *Psalm* 118:24-27, meaning "Save us now." The chief priests and the scribes protested this acclamation, for it was a prayer that God protect and prosper Jesus as king and son of David, implying He was the Messiah!

Later that afternoon, Jesus spoke to the crowd. Among them, there were some Greeks who had come up to worship at the feast. They came to Philip and said, *"Sir, we would like to see Jesus"* (*Jn.* 12:20-21). They approached Philip, probably because his name was Greek and his hometown was Bethsaida, which bordered the ten Greek cities of northern Palestine. Philip went to Andrew, whose name is also Greek. Both of them went to Jesus to ask for this interview.

This request of the Gentiles was one of the great moments in the life of Jesus. For this incident marks the first hint that Jesus meant the Gospel to have a worldwide outreach. Ecstatically, He cried out, "The hour has come for the Son of Man to be glorified." "The hour has come," that is, the moment has come to begin the action that will lead to bringing the Gospel to the Gentiles. And His glory was precisely this: to draw all men to Himself, not just His countrymen.

And the action that was to begin this worldwide evangelization was to be His death. *"Unless the grain of wheat falls to the earth and dies, it remains just a grain of wheat. But if it dies, it produces much fruit"* (*Jn.* 12:20).

Afterwards, Jesus retired to Bethany, to the home of Martha and Mary, where He stayed that Sunday night.

MONDAY IN HOLY WEEK, APRIL 3, A.D. 30

On the next morning, Jesus wended His way back to the city. He seemed to be in a volcanic mood. He was hungry. Seeing a fig tree by the roadside, He went to it and found only leaves but no figs. Aloud, in the hearing of the apostles, He cursed it, saying, *"May no one ever eat of your fruit again!"* (*Mk.* 11:12-14).

Then, according to the synoptics, He entered the city and cleansed the temple. Lagrange and Riciotti believe that there was only one cleansing of the temple and that this occurred at the time given by John, namely, at the beginning of Jesus' ministry (*Jn.* 2:13-17). If there had been a second cleansing of the temple, and it occurred here, so short a time before His Passion, it seems very strange that no mention of this was made at the trial of Jesus. Like Lagrange and Riciotti, I also opt for a single cleansing (see pg. 15).

When evening came, Jesus returned to Bethany and spent the Monday night there (*Mk.* 11:19).

TUESDAY IN HOLY WEEK, APRIL 4, A.D. 30

The next morning, Jesus returned once more to Jerusalem. On the way they passed the fig tree He had cursed the day before. It had withered to its roots. Peter remarked, *"Rabbi, look! The fig tree that you cursed has withered"* (*Mk.* 11:21).

This strange action of Jesus (the only time He worked a miracle not from the kindness of His heart) was a parable in action. The withering of the fig tree was meant to impress on the apostles the finality of Israel's fate. The fig tree stood for Israel. Israel produced no fruits. When He had entered Jerusalem the previous Sunday, the crowds shouted when they should have repented—leaves, no figs. Israel would wither away. It was doomed. Of course this was unthinkable to His Galileans, the most nationalistic of God's people. To help them cope with this prophecy, Jesus told them to have faith in God and to pray.

Jesus further demonstrated how blind and deaf the religious leaders were by the parable of the Two Sons (*Mt.* 21:28-32). Jesus likened them to the second son, who rejected his father's will. *Vox et praetera nihil:* they were all talk and nothing else, and so merited the fate of the fig tree.

He went further to point out that their malice exceeded even that of their ancestors by the allegory of the Tenant Farmers (*Mk.* 12:1-12). Their ancestors murdered the servants of God, but they would murder the only Son of the owner of the vineyard. In a supreme appeal to their conscience, Jesus reminded them that God was indeed patient, but that He was also just: should they not shape up, their vineyard would be forfeited.

When the people heard this, they exclaimed, "Let it not be so!" With a look of pity and love, Jesus turned to the crowds. He was speaking in the southern part of the temple, the Royal Porch; from there, He could point to the corner stone on the southeast wall, the pinnacle of the temple. Jesus said to the people that the leaders have rejected the corner stone, and so have spelled out their own destruction. The people now must make their choice; if they reject Him, they reject the mercy of God.

On the feast of St. John the Baptist, Augustine said,

"Truth begets hatred; and a woman's hatred led to his murder." Likewise, the incontestable truth spoken by Jesus moved His enemies to plot how they might lay hands on Him. After His enemies had left the crowds to spin their plot against Jesus, He told the people the parable of the Marriage Feast, hoping to win them at least (*Mt.* 22:1-14). The point of His parable was "Many are invited, but few are chosen." He hoped this parable would shake them out of any smugness: would make them see that not all the saved would be Israelites; nor would all the Israelites be saved! He was telling them that to be one of God's chosen people is not enough; rather the wedding garment of grace and good works is required!

In the meanwhile, the unyielding enemies of Jesus, the legalistic Pharisees, their rivals the rich and worldly Sadduccees, and the Herodians, banned together to hatch three subtle questions to ensnare Jesus in His speech. One was about paying tribute to Caesar; a second, about the resurrection; and a third, about the Great Commandment. *"Softer than butter was their speech, but war was in their heart. Their words were smoother than oil, but they were drawn swords"* (*Ps.* 55:22).

TRIBUTE TO CAESAR (*Mk.* 12:13-17)

So with honeyed words, His enemies said: "Teacher, you are a truthful man and are not concerned about what others think. Is it lawful to pay the census tax to Caesar or not?" They had hoped to gore Jesus on the horns of a dilemma. To refuse tribute to Caesar would implicate Him in treason; to endorse tribute would alienate the people awaiting a Messiah to free Israel from foreign domination. Brilliantly, Jesus merely asked for a coin. "Whose image and inscription is on it?" He asked. They replied, "Caesar's." So Jesus said to them, "Repay to Caesar what belongs to Caesar." Then Jesus went one step further. The image of God is stamped on every soul; so the other side of the coin, He said, is to "Repay to God what belongs to God."

THE SADDUCEES AND THE RESURRECTION (*Mk*. 12:19-27)

Still, no conversions here. Instead, the Sadduccees, who denied the resurrection of the dead, sought to embarrass Him (as they always had the Pharisees, who believed in the resurrection of the dead), by posing a loaded question, supposedly unanswerable. The case had to do with a woman who had had seven husbands. The question was: "At the resurrection whose wife would she be?" They felt this would stump Jesus, as it always had the Pharisees; and thus greatly diminish Jesus' credibility and popularity.

Unflustered, Jesus simply pointed out that they did not know the scriptures or the power of God. "When they rise from the dead, they neither marry nor are given in marriage, but they are like the angels in heaven." In the kingdom to come, there would be no death and so no need for marriage. There will be love but no sexual desire.

THE GREAT COMMANDMENT (*Mk*. 12:28-34)

Jesus' masterful reply elated the Pharisees, who had never been able to give a satisfactory answer to the Sadduccees' conundrum of the woman with seven husbands. As a result, some of them gathered about Jesus; and, in a spirit of friendliness, one of the scribes asked Him, "Which is the first of all the commandments?"

In His answer Jesus showed that He was orthodoxy itself, that He was no law-breaker. For His answer was Israel's great confession of faith in God, the *Shema: "Hear, O Israel! The Lord our God is Lord alone! You shall love the Lord your God with all your heart."* Then seeking to turn His enemies from their wicked plots, Jesus continued, *"And the second is this: You shall love your neighbor as yourself."*

Seeing their good will, Jesus endeavored to lead them to the truth about Himself. His sole concern was to save their souls, not to worst them in argument. So He asked them, *"What is your opinion about the Messiah? Whose son is he?"* (*Mt.* 22:42). They answered, "David's." Then Jesus explained the great Messianic *Psalm 109* to them. It was in vain; they reverted to their old prejudices, clammed up, and closed their minds to the truth. No one dared "to ask him any more questions."

Dismayed by this hardness, Jesus sadly, lovingly, without any vindictiveness, warned the people about the hypocrisy of their leaders. Since they had to depend on them for their knowledge of the Mosaic Law, Jesus told them to listen to them as teachers, but not to imitate them, for at heart they were hypocrites and their holiness a mere sham.

Turning to His disciples who were to replace these rabbis, Jesus told them not to seek personal glory. *"Call no one on earth your father; you have but one Father in heaven"* (*Mt.* 23:9).

Often this statement is used to condemn the Catholic practice of calling priests "father." Jesus wasn't finding fault with the term "father." What He was doing was rebuking the Pharisees for their indomitable pride, their putting themselves above God—usurping His authority. Such as these, He said, will be humbled, for "whoever exalts himself will be humbled."

To interpret this statement of Jesus literally is absurd. God Himself said, "Honor your father and your mother." St. Paul wrote: *"You have countless guides to Christ, yet you do not have many fathers for I became your father in Christ Jesus through the gospel"* (*1 Cor.* 4:15).

Catholics lovingly delight in calling their priests "father," because for them a priest is truly a spiritual father: he gives divine life at Baptism, nourishes it at Holy Mass, and restores it, if lost, by the Sacrament of Reconciliation.

HYPROCRISY OF THE SCRIBES AND PHARISEES

The end to Jesus' earthly life was fast approaching. There was no longer time for gentle persuasion. Jesus took off the gloves and lashed out against the scribes and Pharisees, against their false religious spirit, which was responsible for the moral ruin of the nation. They were hirelings, thieves, who cared not for the sheep. So, the Good Shepherd leveled seven woes against them, His vehemence like thunder and lightning exposing their hypocrisy (see pg. 102).

The word "woe" often occurs in prophetic and apocalyptic literature. It expresses horror at evil and grief over the punishment awaiting the evildoers. Jesus never gloried in putting down people; He had come to call sinners. Hence His woes are more like lamentations than condemnations.

Four woes were directed against the teachings of the Pharisees—blind guides leading the people to the pit.

They prevented people from entering the kingdom of God by substituting their teachings for God's truth (1st Woe).

They corrupted their converts by leading them to their brand of religion, not God's (2nd Woe).

They, in their greed, devoured the property and means of widows (3rd Woe).

They nullified oaths by the technique of evasion (4th Woe).

The next three woes bewailed the fact that the scribes and Pharisees were themselves sinners.

They had lost all sense of proportion: straining gnats and swallowing camels—focusing on little things and neglecting the important things (5th Woe).

They valued the outward show and neglected the heart. They were slaves to human respect, concerned only about what people thought of them (6th Woe).

They were like whited tombs. Contact with dead bodies, they believed, even when one is unaware of it, caused ritual impurity (*Num.* 19:11-22). That was why every March, just before the feast of the Passover, the tombs just outside Jerusalem were whitewashed. This made it easy for pilgrims coming from afar to spot them. Thus they could avoid touching them and keep themselves undefiled.

The whitewashed tombs created a lovely picture outside of Jerusalem. Jesus said that the scribes and Pharisees were like those tombstones: nice to look at on the outside, but full of dead men's bones on the inside.

The history of Israel, from beginning to end, that is, from Abel to Zechariah, was a history of rejection of God and the murder of the God-fearing. The great tragedy now was that the scribes and Pharisees were even worse, for they would kill the greatest of the prophets, their hope—the Messiah—and thus doom the nation (7th Woe).

On this ultimate note of warning, Jesus ended His public ministry. From now on, only His disciples would remain with Him. When He left Galilee, Jesus pronounced woes over Corazain, Bethsaida, and Capernaum, so now, as He left Jerusalem, He wept over the city. *"Jerusalem, Jerusalem,...how many times I yearned to gather your children together, as a hen gathers her young under her wings, but you were unwilling! Behold, your house will be abandoned, desolate"* (*Mt.* 23:37-38).

THE WIDOW'S MITE

The crowds dispersed and Jesus walked with His disciples toward the Golden Gate. As He was leaving the temple court, He cast one more lingering look at the temple. Through the Gate Beautiful, He saw the women's court with its 13 trumpet-shaped receptacles to receive offerings for the temple upkeep. The rich were dropping their heavy coins into the receptacles. They rang out as metal hit metal, a trumpet call to all to see their generosity. Our Lord had said, "When you give alms, do not blow a trumpet before you, like hypocrites."

At that moment, a poor widow unobtrusively came to the coffers and put into one of them two small coins worth only a few cents, that barely made a tinkle. Pointing her out to the disciples, Jesus said she had given more than the rich. God wants people, not their money. The religious value of an act is in the intention. The only gift that pleases God is the heart (*Mk.* 12:41-44).

Sixty years later, when St. John wrote his Gospel, he could see in hindsight that the unbelief of the people had been due to their perverse dispositions (*Jn.* 12:37-50).

JESUS FORETELLS THE DESTRUCTION OF JERUSALEM AND ITS TEMPLE

As Jesus and His small group of followers were leaving the temple, one of them, probably Peter, trying to lift up His spirits by showing Him how indestructible the temple was, said, *"Look, teacher, what stones and what buildings!"* (*Mk.* 13:1). Some of the white stones of the walls were fifty feet long, sixteen high, and twenty-four thick, exquisitely carved; the pillars of the porches were forty feet tall; the roof of the sanctuary was covered with plates of gold that glistened and gleamed in the setting sun—there was nothing like this on the shores of the Lake of Galilee.

Jesus was not cheered. He knew only too well all would be destroyed. *"Amen, I say to you, there will not be left here a stone upon another stone that will not be thrown down."* This prophecy was literally fulfilled in A.D. 70 when Titus captured Jerusalem and burned the temple to the ground.

That silenced them all. Without saying a word, they crossed the brook of Kidron and headed up the Mount of Olives for Bethany. At the summit of the Mount, Jesus stopped but the apostles went on. However, Peter, James, John, and Andrew came back to be with Jesus. They asked

Him when these things would happen. Would there be any signs, clues? Peter was thinking not only of the end of Jerusalem, but also of the end of the world, for he could not conceive of a world without Jerusalem.

Jesus made no attempt to distinguish the two events. He spoke first only of Jerusalem. He warned them of false prophets and of persecution. And He urged them to be patient and to be about their business. The only sign He gave them was to know that when the Roman army begins to march on the city, its end is near (*Lk.* 21:20). Then Christians should flee to the mountains.

Isaiah used the imagery of sun, moon and stars for the fall of Babylon. Jesus used it to describe the fall of the new Babylon, Jerusalem. The fall of Jerusalem was in one sense a great disaster, but in another a great blessing, for it ushered in the Messianic era. The fall of Jerusalem marked the victory of Christianity over Judaism.

Jesus concluded with the parable of the Fig Tree: when its leaves appear, you know summer is near; likewise, when these signs appear, know that the end of Jerusalem is near. Then, Jesus considered the second question asked by the apostles: the time and sign of the Parousia, His Second Coming. He gave no clue as to the time. It was a strict secret, not part of His mission to communicate. However, He made it clear that it would come when least expected.

This was Jesus' farewell utterance to His Church through His four most intimate disciples. His words suggest this: *"What I say to you, I say to all: 'Watch!'"* (*Mk.* 13:37).

THE TEN VIRGINS

At this point Jesus probably got up and resumed the walk to Bethany. As He approached the house of Mary and Martha and saw the lights shining, and Mary and Martha preparing supper for Jesus, the bridegroom, He told the parable of the Wise Virgins. The lesson was to stress once more the need for vigilance.

Once in the house, Jesus told the Parable of the Talents, about the rewards for the faithful and productive servants and the punishment of the wicked servant. He told this probably for Judas' sake, to warn him against burying his talent.

THE GENERAL JUDGMENT

To underscore the urgent need for vigilance, fidelity, and industry, Jesus described the last judgment. The word "judgment" means "separation"; and the last judgment means final separation of good and bad—for all eternity! For the good, everlasting happiness; for the bad, everlasting fire (*Mt.* 25:31-46). On a similar chord the Apostles' Creed ends: "I believe in life everlasting."

On this sobering note of everlasting life, in Heaven or in hell, Jesus concluded His teachings and retired to the Mount of Olives to spend the night (*Lk.* 21:37-38).

WEDNESDAY IN HOLY WEEK, APRIL 5, A.D. 30

The Sanhedrin had plotted to apprehend Jesus after the Passover Feast. However, the sudden and unexpected offer of Judas to betray his Master caused them to reverse their decision. They paid Judas 30 pieces of silver and *"from that time on he looked for an opportunity to hand him over"* (*Mt.* 26:15-16).

Jesus, aware of all that was happening, spent Wednesday at Bethany and calmly set about to prepare for the Passover on Thursday.

THE EASTER TRIDUUM

Jesus redeemed us all and gave perfect glory to God through His paschal mystery: dying He destroyed our death and rising He restored our life. With the Easter Triduum—His passion, death, and resurrection—Jesus culminated His earthly life.

Chapter 12

Maundy Thursday, April 6, A.D. 30

"On the first day of the Feast of Unleavened Bread, when the Jews sacrificed the Passover Lamb, his disciples said to Jesus, 'Where do you want us to go and prepare for you to eat the Passover?'" (Mk. 14:12).

Jesus spoke cryptically, to prevent any premature arrest. He told Peter and John, not Judas, who would normally do this, to make the preparations by following a man carrying a pitcher of water, an unusual thing, for ordinarily only women did this. They were to ask the master of the house which the man entered, "Where is the guest room where our Master may eat the Passover with His disciples?"

The master was probably the father of John Mark; it was someone who was a fervent follower of Jesus. His name was purposefully concealed for the same reason that the synoptic writers, Matthew, Mark, and Luke, omitted the story of the resurrection of Lazarus, to forestall any reprisals on the friends of Jesus.

The preparations were completed that day and the supper took place that same evening.

THE LAST SUPPER

The first question about the Last Supper is, "Was it a Passover meal?" Very likely it was. The question the disciples asked Jesus was about preparing for a Passover meal (*Mk.* 14:12; *Lk.* 22:7-8; *Mt.* 26:17).

If it were not a Passover meal, why was it eaten in Jerusalem and not in Bethany, where Jesus had been staying

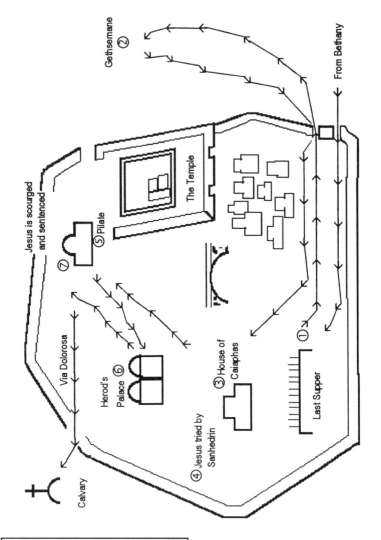

The Last Supper, Arrest, Trials, and Crucifixion

(*Mk.* 11:11)? Why the four cups of wine at the meal (*Luke* 22:17)? Why an evening meal (*Mk.* 14:17)? Why the dipping in the charoseth sauce (*Mk.* 14:20)? Why the concern for the poor, a standard feature of a Passover meal (*Jn.* 13:29)? Why the talk about the covenant of blood (*Lk.* 2:20)? Only in the context of a Passover supper do the words and actions of Jesus at His Last Supper make sense.

The Passover meal memorialized two of the greatest events in Israel's history: first, their liberation—of their firstborn from death by the blood of the lamb, and of the people from Egyptian slavery; and secondly, their Covenant with God on Mt. Sinai.

The bitter herbs and the roasted lamb recalled the liberation from death and slavery. The drinking of four cups of wine at various points during the meal commemorated the Covenant God made with them on Mt. Sinai.

These four cups of wine recalled the four promises God made to the Hebrews on the eve of their exodus from Egypt (*Ex.* 6:6-7): "I will free you from the forced labor of the Egyptians" (the cup of consecration); "I will rescue you . . . with mighty acts" (the cup of proclamation); "I will take you as my own people" (the cup of benediction); and "You shall have me as your God" (the final cup of benediction or thanksgiving).

The Passover meal can best be described within the framework of these four cups.

The Supper usually started about 6:00 P.M. and generally did not go beyond midnight.

First Cup (*Lk.* 22:17). The meal began when the head of the family poured wine into a cup and then recited a prayer of blessing upon the feast and upon the wine. After tasting the wine, he passed it along to the others to drink.

Then, after washing his hands three times, he took some bitter herbs, dipped them into the thick sauce (charoseth) and ate them—there was one dish of sauce for every three persons. He did the same with one of the three loaves of unleavened bread *(matzoh),* which was broken into small pieces *(Lk.* 22:19), to signify the bread of affliction in Egypt. The small pieces reminded them that a slave never had a whole loaf of bread to eat, but only a fragment. Finally, the roasted lamb was brought in.

Second Cup. The cup was then filled a second time and the youngest of the group asked, "Why is this night different from all other nights?" At the Last Supper, perhaps John did this.

The head of the family responded by explaining the symbolic meaning of the meal: salt water, for tears and the Red Sea; broken bread, for affliction and poverty as slaves; and the lamb, for liberation.

The first part of the *Hallel (Psalm* 112-113:8) was sung. Hallel means a hymn of praise. Then the second cup was taken.

After hands were washed, the normal ceremonial before a meal, everyone took his place for the main course. At this juncture a quarrel broke out. It seems that Judas started it by claiming the honor of sitting next to Jesus *(Jn.* 13:2). John, one of the sons of thunder, probably was party to this quarrel *(Lk.* 22:24-30).

This debate for precedence dismayed Jesus. His exhortations to humility, His own example—all seemed to have fallen on deaf ears; human nature does not change easily. So this time, He gave them a dramatic example of humility by washing their feet, the task of the lowest slave in a household *(Jn.* 13:1-20).

When Jesus had finished, He put on His garments again and resumed His place at table. The table was U-shaped. Divans were arranged around the outer edge of the U. Most likely Jesus occupied the divan at the center of the curve.

Diners reclined with their heads toward the table. Peter

was probably to the left of Jesus; John to His right, since he leaned on the breast of Jesus; and Judas to John's right, near enough so that Jesus could dip His bread in the sauce and hand it to the traitor (*Jn.* 13: 26). Da Vinci has this arrangement in his Last Supper painting. Others put Judas to the left of Jesus and Peter to the right of John.

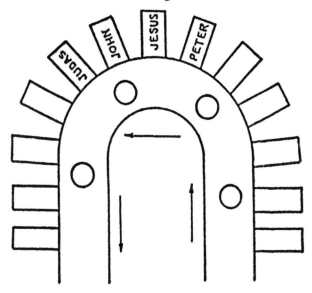

Diagram of the seating arrangement of the Last Supper.

The main course began with grace. Pieces of the broken bread were passed around and dipped into the thick charoseth sauce. During this action, Jesus announced that "the one to whom I hand the morsel after I have dipped it" would betray Him. He handed the morsel to Judas. After that, Satan entered him, and Judas left to betray Jesus (*Jn.* 13:26-30).

THE INSTITUTION OF THE HOLY EUCHARIST

The lamb was eaten. Hands were washed and the rest of the bread was passed around. Perhaps it was here that Jesus consecrated the bread.

Then the **Third Cup** (the cup of benediction) was filled, blessed, and all drank from it. It was probably this third cup that Jesus consecrated (*1 Cor.* 10:16).

What effect these words and actions had on the apostles we don't know. But surely they must have remembered the great promise Jesus had made after the multiplication of the loaves and His walking on water—the promise of giving them His flesh to eat and His blood to drink. This apparently cannibalistic saying had alienated everyone but the apostles (*Jn.* 6). Perhaps, they thought Jesus had forgotten His promise. But on this night when He unexpectedly took bread and wine saying, *"This is my body"*; *"This is my blood,"* the enigma of *Jn.* 6:52-58 became clear to them.

Twenty-five years later (A.D. 57), St. Paul wrote to the Corinthians (*1 Cor.* 11:23-29) that the Eucharist was a permanent rite in which the faithful who shared in it ate the real Body and drank the real Blood of Christ.

THE INSTITUTION OF THE PRIESTHOOD

Of course some deny that Jesus intended what He had done to be established as a permanent rite in the Church. But with the words *"Do this in remembrance of me"* (*Lk.* 22:19), He ordained a priesthood, empowered to make present His redemptive act till the end of time.

If a mother sends a child to the supermarket to get groceries, the presumption is that she gives the child the money to pay for them. Likewise in commissioning His apostles to do what He had done, the presumption is He empowered them to do what He had commanded. Nor did He mean this power to be for them alone, but for all their successors. Thus after His ascension into Heaven, the apostles appointed Matthias to succeed Judas and conferred upon him the same powers they enjoyed.

THE NEW COMMANDMENT

Like an afterglow of the Eucharist, Jesus addressed His

own in terms of endearment, "My children . . ." Then He commanded them to love: "I give you a new commandment. . . . As I have loved you, so you also should love one another." The commandment was new, because the standard was new: love others, not as one loves oneself, but as God loves; that is, unconditionally (*Jn.* 13:31-35). The Latin word for commandment was *"mandatum."* In the Dark Ages when Latin was corrupted, "mandatum" became *"maundatum"*; hence Maundy Thursday.

This new commandment was to be their identification papers—"By this shall all know you are my disciples."

Tertullian said when the pagans saw the Christians, they exclaimed: "See how they love one another" (pagans hated one another). "See how they are ready to die for one another" (pagans were always ready to kill one another).

St. Clement of Alexandria stated confidently: "You can always know a pagan by the ugly pleasures in which he indulges, and a heretic by his bickering and quarrelsomeness, and a Christian by his happiness and love."

To show how He loved, Jesus went on to say that even though they would deny Him, He would still come to them, pray for them, care for them. Peter protested he would never deny His Master. Jesus answered solemnly, *"Amen, I say to you, this very night before the cock crows twice you will deny me three times"* (*Mk.* 14:30). This was too much for Peter; he burst into a torrent of protests. Jesus simply told Peter that He had prayed for him that his faith may not fail and that once converted he was to strengthen his brothers (*Lk.* 22:31-32).

Still they did not understand. Deny Him? Why, they protested, if need be, we will fight for you—see, we have two swords. With infinite patience, Jesus must have smiled sadly and said, "Enough!"

They were troubled. So this changeless lover comforted them in a beautiful discourse beginning, "Let not your hearts be troubled, for my departure is not abandonment. I will not leave you orphans. I will ask the Father to give you the Spirit of Truth who will be with you always. Peace I leave with you; my peace I give you" (*Jn.* 14).

Fourth Cup. Finally, the cup is filled a fourth time. The rest of the *Hallel* is sung (*Ps.* 115-118), followed by the *Great Hallel, Psalm* 136. After that, the fourth cup is drunk, followed by two prayers, the final grace. (See Note at end of chapter).

After the fourth cup, Jesus said, *"Get up, let us go"* (*Jn.* 14:31).

JESUS' FAREWELL ADDRESS

If they headed immediately toward the Garden of Olives, they could have seen the golden doors of the temple, embossed with a vine, the symbol of Israel, glittering in the bright light of the paschal moon. And this could have prompted Jesus' discourse on the Vine and the Branches (*Jn.* 15).

More likely, however, they went directly from the supper room to the rooftop. Our Lord's "I am the true vine," very probably was inspired by the many references to the vine at the drinking of the four cups, for instance, "Blessed art Thou, Eternal, our God, Ruler of the universe, Creator of the fruit of the vine." Jesus said "I am the true vine"—the true vine, true, not false, as Israel had become. "Remain in me." For as St. Augustine wrote: *Aut vitis, aut ignis*— "Either the vine or the fire" (*Jn.* 15:1-17).

Jesus foretold that the world's response to those who remain in the Vine would be hatred and persecution. Forewarned is forearmed. But better still, Jesus comforted them with the promise that the Advocate would come to them—*"He will convict the world in regard to sin and righteousness and condemnation"* (*Jn.* 16:8).

Like a great lawyer, He will convict the world of sin—in

the lawcourt of their hearts He will make the world realize that it had sinned in rejecting Jesus; of righteousness—He will make the world see that righteousness triumphed, for even though Jesus died in disgrace, He rose from the dead and returned to the Father; of condemnation—for He will make the world see that the death of Jesus has chained Satan, limiting His power and activity in the world. As Augustine said, "He who gets bit by a chained dog has nobody to blame but himself."

Jesus concluded His discourse with a sublime priestly prayer for unity. Unity would be the hallmark of His Church.

First, He prayed for Himself—"Father, the hour has come. Give glory to your son . . ."; then He prayed for His disciples—"I pray for them. I do not pray for the world but for the ones you have given me . . . keep them in your name so that they may be one . . . keep them from the evil one. . . . Consecrate them in the truth"; and then He prayed "for those who will believe in Him through their word, so that they may all be one as you, Father, are in me and I in you . . ." (*Jn.* 17).

"*When he had prayed thus, Jesus went out with his disciples across the Kidron valley to where there was a garden . . .* (*Jn.* 18:1). It was about 9:00 P.M.

Note

Scott Hahn, a minister converted to the Catholic faith, believes the Fourth Cup was omitted at the supper. He quotes the words of Jesus after the consecration of the bread and the wine: "*Amen I say to you, I shall not drink again the fruit of the vine until the day when I drink it new in the kingdom of God.*" Right after saying that, Mark says, "*Then, after singing a hymn, they went out to the Mount of Olives*" (*Mk.* 14:25-26). Then in the Garden Jesus kneels and prays three times: "*Abba, Father,. . . . Take this cup away from me"* (*Mk.* 14:36). This cup, not necessarily the cup of suffering, but the fourth cup.

On Calvary when wine drugged with myrrh is offered Him, He would not take it (*Mk.* 15:23).

St. John describes the sacrifice of Jesus as the fulfillment of the Passover. Thus he mentions the seamless garment, which the priest wore at Passover (*Jn.* 19:23), and that none of His bones were broken, for the lamb of the Passover had to be unblemished and with no broken bones (*Jn.* 19:36).

Then John records the words of Jesus "I thirst." This Jesus uttered, not because He had not been thirsty before, but to fulfill the Scriptures. After His cry, a sponge was soaked in wine and was put on a sprig of hyssop (hyssop was used to sprinkle the blood of the lamb on the doorposts at the first Passover) and put up to His mouth. This time, Jesus took the wine and said, "It is finished" (*Jn.* 19:28-30): the fourth cup.

To what did the "it" refer to? "It is finished"—what is finished? The Passover sacrifice. The sacrifice begun in the upper room with the institution of the Eucharist and completed on the cross. But it was still not over.

We all must share in the sacrifice. That is why in *Revelation* 5:6, Jesus appears as the Lamb slain but standing alive, for the sacrifice continues in Heaven—". . . *He lives forever to make intercession for us"* (*Heb.* 7:25); and it continues on earth in the Mass—*"For our paschal lamb, Christ has been sacrificed. Therefore let us celebrate the feast"* (*1 Cor.* 5:7-8). We celebrate it by the Mass, offering Him and ourselves to the Father and receiving Him in Holy Communion to establish our union with the Father and with one another.

Chapter 13

Good Friday

GETHSEMANE

"Then Jesus came with them to a place called Gethsemane" (*Mt.* 26:36). Gethsemane was an olive orchard on the western slope of the Mount of Olives. Like the Cenacle, this garden probably belonged to the father of John Mark. Two things happened in Gethsemane: Jesus' agony (*Mt.* 26:36-46), and His betrayal and arrest (*Mt.* 26:47-56).

The Agony of Jesus (*Mt.* 26:36-44)

Here in the garden, Jesus "began to be troubled and distressed." He said to his disciples, "My soul is sorrowful even to death" (*Mk.* 14:33-34). "He was in such agony and He prayed so fervently that His sweat became like drops of blood falling on the ground" (*Lk.* 22:44). This is a phenomenon not unknown in medicine. Naturally, Luke the physician was interested in this. He alone mentions the angel and the bloody sweat.

The causes of this agony, intense enough to bring on death, were threefold: thoughts of the shame and pain of His sufferings and death on the morrow; the heartache arising from the realization of the futility for so many of so much suffering; and the sins of all mankind.

In His agony, Jesus fell to the ground and prayed. Jews prayed standing; His falling to the ground gives some indication of the terrible strain He was under. He asked His Father to let the cup pass from Him if possible. It was not

143

possible. Luke alone tells us that His Father sent Him an angel to comfort and strengthen Him.

Still, after His sufferings and death, the Father did answer His prayers by raising Him from the dead. *"In the days when he was in the flesh, he offered prayers and supplication with loud cries and tears to the one who was able to save him from death, and he was heard because of his reverence"* (*Heb.* 5:7). It was not possible for Jesus not to drink the cup of suffering and death; but after death came resurrection, the conquest of eternal death. "He was heard because of his reverence." In the words of the Psalmist: *"O Lord, I cried to you for help and you, my God, have healed me. O Lord, you have raised my soul from the dead, restored me to life . . ."* (*Ps.* 30:3-4).

So too when we pray in times of trial, prayer may not take away the trial, but it will give us the power to cope with it and draw good from it, as Jesus did from His cross. Like Him, we too must ever have recourse to One who is our Father and trust Him.

> He knows, He loves, He cares—
> Nothing this truth can dim;
> He gives the very best to those,
> Who leave the choice with Him.

The agony lasted a long time; probably past midnight. The three apostles, at first terribly distressed by what they saw, sank gradually into a kind of sleep induced by sorrow and fatigue. When Jesus finally came to them, He mildly remarked, "My little ones, is this a good time to sleep? Don't you realize that the traitor is here?"

The Betrayal and Arrest of Jesus, Friday, April 7, A.D. 30, about 12:30 A.M. (*Mt.* 26:47-56)

Judas was familiar with our Lord's habits. Jesus was wont to pray in Gethsemane. Moreover, the Passover had to be celebrated in Jerusalem or its immediate environs, so Judas knew Jesus would not have gone to Bethany. A great crowd came with Judas, with swords and clubs—a recognition of the great power of Jesus. They had lanterns and torches, even though the moon was full; perhaps they expected Jesus to be hiding in some cave or ravine. They were taken by surprise when Jesus came out to meet them. Judas got nervous and went right up and kissed Him several times.

Oh, how this must have grieved the heart of Jesus. Even at this last hour, He still called him "friend," hoping to bring him to his senses. The words of the Psalmist express the feelings of Jesus: *"If an enemy had reviled me, I could have borne it... But you, my other self, my companion and my bosom friend!"* (*Ps.* 55:13-14).

When assassins were stabbing Julius Caesar, he fought like a lion until he saw his friend Brutus stab him too. That took the heart out of him. Unable to believe his eyes, Caesar cried out, *"Et tu, Brute?*And you, Brutus, my friend? Then fall, Caesar!"* Far more painful and devastating to Jesus was the betrayal of Judas.

After the Judas kiss, they seized Jesus. Poor, bewildered Simon Peter drew his sword and cut off the right ear of Malchus, a servant of the high priest. Jesus immediately stepped in and told Peter to put his sword back into its sheath. To protect Peter, He healed Malchus and ordered the soldiers to let His followers go (*Jn.* 18:10-11).

Even in this frightful situation, Jesus' sole concern was not for Himself, but for His disciples. All the disciples left Him. Only a certain young teenager, perhaps John Mark, whose father owned the garden, followed Him. Perhaps John Mark had been sent to sleep in a shed in the Garden because there were so many guests at his home: Mary and the other women who had taken care of the Last Supper meal. John Mark had a linen night shirt on, which the well-to-do wore. When John Mark was seized, he left his linen night shirt behind and fled away naked. So Jesus was abandoned by His last friend: a lad without any clothes! (*Mk.* 14:51-52).

The Trial of Jesus

In the garden Jesus let himself be bound. He was led up the Kidron valley to the Fountain Gate at the southeast corner of the city, up the graded road to Caiaphas' house in the southwestern quarter of the city. Then, Jesus underwent three different judicial examinations.

The Trial Before Annas

Annas had been deposed as high priest in A.D. 15, but still retained great authority. Five of his sons, a grandson and his son-in-law, Caiaphas, succeeded him. Caiaphas was high priest from A.D. 18 to 36.

Annas probably lived in the same palace as Caiaphas. The building complex was a large rectangle: on one side were Annas' quarters; on the opposite side, Caiaphas'; in between was a courtyard which could be shared by both. Jesus' trial in Annas' quarters was unofficial and simply interrogative.

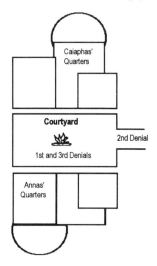

During the trial before Annas, Peter was warming himself at the fire in the courtyard with the enemies of Jesus. More in a bantering way than in malice, a maidservant said to Peter, "You were with the Galilean." Peter denied he was. And the cock crowed a first time. At that time of the year, roosters never crowed before 2:30 A.M.

Peter felt uneasy, so he left the courtyard and went to the arched gateway at the entrance to the courtyard. While he was there, Jesus was led across the courtyard to the quarters of Caiaphas. In the meantime, at the entrance another maidservant ran into Peter accidentally and continued the banter that had been going on in the courtyard. This time Peter denied knowing Jesus with an oath.

The Trial Before Caiaphas

Upset, Peter returned to the fire in the courtyard. He could probably see the judicial proceedings against Jesus in the upper story of Caiaphas' house. Maybe during the quest for witnesses to testify against Jesus, someone pointed out Peter. His Galilean dress and his speech gave him away. Even a relative of Malchus asked him, "Did I not see you in the garden with the Galilean?" Peter cursed vehemently and denied the overwhelming evidence. The cock crowed a second time; it was about 4:00 A.M.

At about this time the trial reached its climax. Desperate, Caiaphas asked Jesus point blank, "Are you the Messiah, the son of the Blessed One?" Jesus answered, "I am." Caiaphas tore his garments and accused Jesus of blasphemy. Then *"they all condemned him as deserving of death. Some began to spit on him. They blindfolded him and struck him (Mk.* 14:64-65).

This trial before Caiaphas was illegal, because it was held at night, because it was held in the high priest's home instead of in the temple wing, and because it was conducted by the high priest when he should have been presiding at it as an unbiased judge. Moreover, false witnesses had been admitted; and their testimonies conflicted so that the case should have been thrown out (*Mk.* 14:53-64).

But these minions of the powers of darkness threw justice to the winds. On His way to their prison, Jesus crossed the courtyard and saw Peter. He looked at Peter, and that look brought Peter to his senses and Jesus' words to his mind, *" 'Before the cock crows twice you will deny me three times.' Peter went out and wept bitterly"* (*Mk.* 14:66-72).

Though Peter's denials are said to be three, it does not mean that these were just three single acts—a question and an answer. More likely each question was followed by much discussion. Peter's denials teach us the danger of presumption (it can be almost as fatal as despair); they teach that *"bad company corrupts good morals"* (*1 Cor.* 15:33); and also the power of repentance. After his denials, Peter no doubt went to John; and John brought him to Mary; and Mary probably took care of the rest.

The Morning Trial Before the Sanhedrin

Early the next morning, the Sanhedrin met again, this time to ratify the death sentence passed against Jesus the night before and to formulate charges that would move Pilate to affirm their verdict. Only the Romans could impose the death penalty. The Sanhedrin did their work in short order.

Ironically, afterwards, many of the members of the Sanhedrin went to the temple to assist at the morning sacrifice, and give thanks to God for their successful case against Jesus.

JUDAS

It was after this morning session that Judas realized the gravity of his sin. It is typical of the strategy of the devil to minimize a crime before its committal then to magnify it beyond all bounds after it has been done. So Judas went to the temple and before the members of the Sanhedrin blurted out, "I've betrayed innocent blood." But he got no satisfaction from them. So he flung the silver pieces on the floor of the priests' court and went out and hanged himself.

The chief priests and rulers had been negotiating to buy a potter's field as a burial place for strangers. The field was located on the southern side of the valley of Hinnon. It was called the potter's field, because its soil was ideal for making pottery. They saw in Judas' money a way to pay for this field. Because the blood of Jesus or the blood of Judas clung to the money, they called the field *"Haceldema,"* the Field of Blood (*Mt.* 27:3-10).

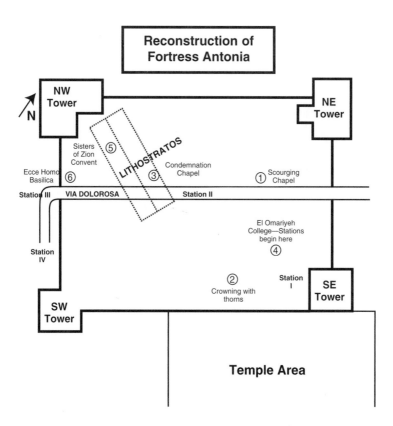

JESUS BEFORE PILATE, FRIDAY MORNING, APRIL 7, AROUND 7:00 A.M. (*Jn.* 18:28)

The Procurator of Judea resided at Caesarea on the Mediterranean. But during the great festivals of the Jews, he moved to Jerusalem to prevent any disturbances. Pontius Pilate was Procurator of Judea for ten years (A.D. 27-36). Pilate was arrogant, imprudent, and an opportunist. He was removed from office in A.D. 36 by Caligula because of his high-handed dealing with the Samaritans. Some say that he was exiled to Mt. Pilatus overlooking Lake Lucerne in Switzerland, and that a few years later, in remorse and despair, he drowned himself in the lake on Mt. Pilatus.

All the events regarding Jesus' trial before Pilate took place in the Fortress Antonia. The public part of the trial was held in the big courtyard called *Lithostratos,* from two Greek words meaning "stone pavement." In Hebrew it was called *Gabbatha* because it was an elevated place. Here Pilate set up the customary curule seat to interrogate the crowd, hear the accusations against Jesus and His defense. Here, too, Pilate presented Jesus after His scourging and said, "Behold the Man!" Here also Pilate finally washed his hands and condemned Jesus to death on the cross.

The private part of Jesus' trial, the interrogations by Pilate, was held in the palace of the Procurator, situated on a rocky platform east of and above the *Lithostratos.* The stairs (*Scala Santa*—"The Holy Stairs") leading from the *Lithostratos* to the palace were, according to a tradition, brought to Rome by St. Helen in 326. Pope Sixtus V, in 1589, transferred the "holy stairs" from the Lateran Palace to the Church of San Salvatore next to the Basilica of St. John Lateran. The stairs may be ascended only on one's knees.

That Good Friday morning Jesus was brought before Pilate, who doubted Caiaphas' charge of sedition. After all, Pilate had his own informers. Then, too, Jesus must have impressed him; no doubt the tribune had reported the Gethsemane affair. Also, Claudia, Pilate's wife, had sent him this message: *"Have nothing to do with that righteous man. I suffered much in a dream today because of him"* (*Mt.* 27:19). Finally, Pilate knew that the Jews had proceeded illegally against Him. So Pilate said to them, *"What charge do you bring against this man?"* (*Jn.* 18:29).

This caught the Jews unawares. They answered vaguely, "We would never hand over a Jew to you if he were innocent." Pilate read into their answer some minor crime, so he told them to judge the case themselves. Then they showed their true colors: they wanted a death sentence. So they leveled three charges against Him: sedition—He misleads the people; rebellion—He opposed paying taxes to Caesar; and treason—He maintains he is the Messiah, a king (*Lk.* 23:2).

Pilate was too well informed to put any credence in the first two charges; he interrogated Jesus about the last charge. "Are you the king of the Jews," he asked. Pilate expected a "No." Jesus distinguished: "A political king? No. My kingdom does not belong to this world. If it did my followers would be fighting to keep me from being handed over to the Jews. A king of truth? Yes" (*Jn.* 18:36-37).

Pilate found no guilt in Jesus worthy of death, so he should have freed Him. But he did not. Judas embodied disloyalty; the Sanhedrin personified duplicity; and Pilate exemplified cowardice. This weakness encouraged the chief priests and elders. They knew they could browbeat Pilate into doing their will by an unbroken chant of accusations. As animals chase retreating objects, so cowardice makes the devil a bully. Pilate was a coward.

Jesus had probably convinced Pilate of His innocence. That was all Pilate needed to know to do his duty. From then on, Jesus remained silent, lest Pilate's guilt be the more increased.

JESUS BEFORE HEROD

To extricate himself from his predicament, Pilate tried to pass the buck. He sent Jesus, a Galilean, to Herod Antipas, Tetrarch of Galilee. Herod was in Jerusalem at the time. To curry favor with the Judeans, the Herodians were accustomed to go to Jerusalem for the feast of the Passover.

Herod was very glad to see Jesus. He had heard so much about Him that his curiosity was aroused. So he received Jesus in state, with Herodias at his side. He questioned Jesus. But Jesus made no answer. Truth is wasted on those who are not sincere.

Deeply humiliated by Jesus' silent treatment, Herod tried to save face by making out that Jesus was an idiot. Among the Romans, anyone canvassing for office always wore a white garment to attest to his spotless character. The Latin word for "white" was *candidus;* hence our word "candidate."

So Herod robed Jesus in white and mocked Him as a candidate for kingship. This was hilarious; to his sycophants it was a stroke of genius—to parade this Jesus as a pretender, canvassing for a throne. So Herod's court joined in, mocking Jesus, spitting on Him and heaping upon Him insult after insult. When they had had their fill, they sent Him back to Pilate.

Before this, Herod and Pilate had been enemies, probably over Pilate's massacre of some Galileans (*Lk.* 13:1). In sending a Galilean to him for judgment, Pilate was acknowledging Herod's right. This healed the breach between them. And that day they became friends. Jesus gave them peace with each other, but that was the only blessing He could give them, for their hearts were not right.

Pilate's problem had been tossed back into his lap. In the meantime, the chief priests and rulers had become more brazen. They felt Pilate owed them for forcing them to traipse through the streets, like fools, to Herod's palace.

They insisted that he make amends by compliance to their demands.

Pilate felt he had yet another way out of his dilemma. On a feast, the governor was accustomed to release to the crowd one prisoner whom they wished. So Pilate brought out a notorious criminal, Barabbas. He even suggested the answer he wanted by asking a leading question: "Do you want me to release to you the king of the Jews?" Not Barabbas, but the king of the Jews.

Knowing that Jesus' arrest was due chiefly to the envy of the religious leaders in Jerusalem, who resented His popularity with the people, and that the people a few days before had hailed Him as king when He rode into Jerusalem, Pilate felt he had every reason now to expect that the crowd would speak in favor of Jesus. Again, he miscalculated. The rulers of the people had persuaded the mob to choose Barabbas.

Three times Pilate spoke to the people, but his want of earnestness only encouraged the mob, and their cries became louder and their demands for Jesus' crucifixion more insistent each time he questioned them. Still determined to avoid the death sentence, Pilate said, *"I shall have him flogged and then release him"* (Lk. 23:16). The scourging was inflicted by the soldiers in some part of their barracks.

JESUS IS SCOURGED AND
CROWNED WITH THORNS (*Jn.* 19:1-3)

Jewish law forbade more than 40 lashes *"lest your kinsman be looked upon as disgraced because of the severity of the beating"* (*Dt.* 25:3). Romans had no limit. Horace, who was none too squeamish, called the instrument used for scourging *horribile flagellum*—"the horrible lash." Romans reserved scourging for slaves; a Roman citizen was beaten with the lictor's rods.

The scourge used on Jesus was not a cat-o'-nine-tails, but

just two thongs tipped with barbell-shaped metal weights at the end of each thong. Flicked by two executioners, with a whip-cracking motion, these bruised the body and sometimes ruptured the skin. According to the shroud of Turin, Jesus' arms were tied above His head; His naked body was beaten over the entire surface. Counting merely the open wounds on the shroud of Turin, Jesus must have received at least sixty lashes.

The scourging is one of the few details of His sufferings of which Jesus spoke (*Mk.* 10:34). In the miraculous picture of Our Lady of Perpetual Help, the instruments of Jesus's passion are held by the angels Gabriel and Michael— among them is the scourge; and Jesus is looking at them in terror, clinging tightly to His Mother.

Pilate had intended by having Jesus scourged to satiate the blood thirst of His enemies. *"I shall have him flogged and then release him"* (*Lk.* 23:16). Release Him? Never! So the scribes and the Pharisees bribed the soldiers to lay on the lash to kill Him by that if needs be. *"Upon my back the plowers ploughed; long did they make their furrows"* (*Ps.* 129:3).

After they were done with Him, they cut the cords and He collapsed into a pool of His own blood. Tertullian says that they kept kicking Him, like a ball, to make Him rise and put on His garments. Then were fulfilled the words: *"I am a worm not a man"* (*Ps.* 22:7); for, like a worm, He was writhing in agony on the ground, the reproach of men.

For some reason or other Pilate was not ready for Jesus after the scourging; thus He was left for some time longer to the mercy of the soldiers. In the *Lithostratos*, some of the flagstones were striated to prevent horses from slipping. At regular intervals there were large shallow gutters to carry rain water to the two large cisterns beneath the pavement.

Most interesting are the games cut into the flagstones These games were played by the Roman soldiers to kill time. One of the games was *Basilicus,* the King's game. The soldiers used to choose a burlesque king, mock him, and then put him to death.

From the Gospels we know that the soldiers decided to play this game on Jesus—after all He claimed to be king of the Jews. So they led Him down a stairway to their barracks.

There, the soldiers gathered the whole cohort, that is, a great number, and stripped Jesus. They put on Him a scarlet cloak, crowned Him with thorns, and stuck a reed in His hands as the scepter of His power.

Then they began to pay Him homage: they bent the knee in mock homage, rose, and took the reed and slammed it down on the crown of thorns, and for a kiss spat in His face. Each soldier of the well-drilled cohort offered this cruel homage in due order, saying in jest, "Hail, King of the Jews!" And they spat on Him and took the reed and kept striking His head (*Mt.* 27:26-30). (See Note at end of chapter.)

PILATE'S LAST RESISTANCE (*Jn.* 19:4-15)

Quite a bit of time elapsed since the soldiers had scourged Jesus. It was about 10:00 to 11:00 A.M. The prophecy: *"He will be handed over to the Gentiles...after they have scourged him they will kill him . . ."* (*Lk.* 18:32) had been abundantly fulfilled. Pilate ordered Jesus to be brought to him. Seeing the pitiable condition to which Jesus had been reduced, he felt confident that the issue would be settled with His release.

He stood on the platform overlooking the *Lithostratos.* Pointing to Jesus, Pilate said to the crowd, *"Ecce Homo!"* (Behold the Man!). It was as if he had said, "Here's the fellow now; the man you feared so much. Is there any point in further violence against one reduced to such a state?" The people were moved. They were silent. But not the chief priests and their guards, wretched slaves without a soul to call their own. These cried out: "Crucify Him, crucify Him!"

Like a child who does not want to do something that the other children are prodding him to do turns on his instigators and says, "You do it!" So Pilate, enraged, turned to them and said: "Take Him yourselves and crucify Him. I find no guilt in Him." He spoke to Jesus again in private. This time Jesus did not speak to him. Pilate, not Jesus, was on trial. Jesus sought to touch his heart, but in vain. With satanic cleverness, the chief priests struck at Pilate's Achilles' heel: his fear of Caesar. "You release Him," they threatened, "and you are no friend of Caesar."

So Pilate caved in. He came with Jesus to the judgment seat set up in the Lithostratos. There, Pilate formally handed Jesus over to His enemies to be crucified. *"It was the preparation day for Passover, and it was about noon"*— eleven or twelve o'clock (*Jn.* 19:14).

THE WAY OF THE CROSS

The exact route of the way of the cross is not absolutely certain. The procession began from the Praetorium in the Fortress of Antonia, in the northwest corner of the temple, and continued in a more or less east-west direction for about three-fifths of a mile to the hill of Golgotha. A white board hung from the neck of each person, telling in large red letters the offense for which each was to die.

St. John suggests that Jesus took up the crossbeam personally, embraced it and balanced it on His shoulder (*Jn.* 19:17). The vertical beam of the cross was fixed permanently at the place of execution. Ordinarily, it was twelve to fifteen feet high so that the feet of the condemned man would be on a level with a man's head. The crossbeam would be fastened to it at some distance from the top, leaving enough room to affix the inscription stating the reason for the execution.

The site for the execution was "the Place of the Skull, in Hebrew called Golgotha." The Latin word for skull is *calvaria;* hence Calvary. It got its name because the mound was shaped like a skull. We call a piece of land jutting out into water "headland" or "cape" ("cape" comes from the Latin word *caput* meaning "head"). Golgotha was located about 400 yards from the Ephraim Gate in the western wall of Jerusalem.

Though Jesus took up the crossbeam by Himself, the burden proved too much for His battered body. He fell. Getting up, He met His mother Mary. He looked at her and she looked at Him and "those looks were as so many arrows that pierced those hearts that loved each other so tenderly."

Mary said nothing. Her love was tough love. She inspired her Jesus to go on, to carry on. She was a veritable tower of David for Him, powerful like an army set in battle array.

When King Alfred had been defeated by the Danes, he was about to give up his struggle with them until he saw the Mother of God and the Christian civilization for which she stood. And she did for him what every great woman does for the man she loves: she did not fight his battle against the Danes for him, that's a man's job, but she inspired him by the love he bore her to make one last effort against Guthrum. Alfred did and won the battle of the White Horse Vale and brought Guthrum and his Danes into the Catholic faith and made England Catholic.

Here is how G.K. Chesterton put it: "Out of the mouth of the Mother of God,/ More than the doors of doom,/ I call for the muster of Wessex men,/ From grassy hamlet or ditch or den,/ To break and be broken, God knows when,/ But I have seen for whom."

Mary may have wanted to help carry the cross (as Simon did), or at least wipe His face (as Veronica did), but she did not. She could not, for she knew the will of the Father, that it was His will that Jesus suffer. As in His agony, He prayed, "Not my will but thine be done," so in this, her agony, Mary prayed too, "Thy will be done."

And as in the garden of Gethsemane, the Father heard Jesus' prayer and sent an angel to comfort Him, so here God heard Mary's prayer and sent three angels to comfort Him: Simon of Cyrene, Veronica, and the daughters of Jerusalem.

Simon of Cyrene

"They pressed into service a passer-by, Simon, a Cyrenian . . . the father of Alexander and Rufus" (Mk. 15:21).

Simon was a Jew from northern Africa, who had come to Jerusalem to celebrate the Passover Feast. We do not know whether he carried the whole crossbeam or just helped Jesus with it. The latter is more likely, since Jesus fell a second and third time afterwards. No matter, Simon must have felt disgraced before everyone at being pressed into this service, and must have cursed his bad luck. Yet the cross was a blessing in disguise. It seems Simon later on received the faith, for his two sons, Alexander and Rufus, had become priests. How then he must have gloried in having shared so intimately in the passion of Jesus!

Veronica

Tradition tells us that a woman, Veronica, drew near to Jesus and wiped His face with her veil. Her home was but a hundred paces from where Simon had been pressed into duty. Some believe that Veronica was the woman, afflicted with hemorrhages for twelve years, whom Jesus had cured on the way to the house of Jairus (*Mk.* 5:25f). Her act was one of love and gratitude and courage.

Jesus rewarded her action by imprinting His face on her veil. The name "Veronica" could mean *vera icon*—"true image." That veil is still preserved in St. Peter's Basilica in Rome. And Veronica is one for the four statues surrounding the high altar at St. Peter's.

The Daughters of Jerusalem

At the Gate of Ephraim in the western wall, leading to Calvary, Jesus fell a second time. Proceeding westward a hundred paces, He met the daughters of Jerusalem, who disturbed the solemn procession with their loud Oriental wails. These women were not the Galilean women who stood by the cross of Jesus; they were Judeans. In the Gospels there is no instance of a woman being hostile to Jesus.

Even here, in the midst of His own indescribable sufferings, Jesus thought of others, of the terrible fate that awaited Jerusalem. He said to the women: *"Daughters of Jerusalem, do not weep for me . . . if these things are done when the wood is green what will happen when it is dry?"* (*Lk.* 23:28-31). If the Victim for sinners suffers so much, how much worse will it be for the sinner!

Possibly the Way of the Cross owes its origin to the Mother of God. In the *Revelations of St. Bridget* (p 67), Our Lady supposedly said: "For all the time that I lived after the Ascension of my Son, I visited the places in which He suffered and showed His wonders." She was accompanied by other Christian women. After her death, Christians began to follow her example, so that the Way of the Cross became the first devotion that Christian pilgrims made in Jerusalem.

If ever you go to Jerusalem, you must make the *Via Dolorosa*.

Via Dolorosa

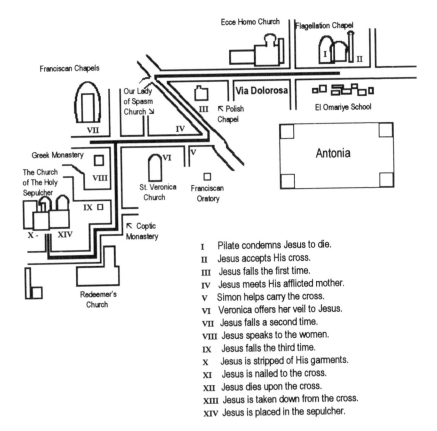

I   Pilate condemns Jesus to die.
II   Jesus accepts His cross.
III   Jesus falls the first time.
IV   Jesus meets His afflicted mother.
V   Simon helps carry the cross.
VI   Veronica offers her veil to Jesus.
VII   Jesus falls a second time.
VIII Jesus speaks to the women.
IX   Jesus falls the third time.
X   Jesus is stripped of His garments.
XI   Jesus is nailed to the cross.
XII   Jesus dies upon the cross.
XIII Jesus is taken down from the cross.
XIV   Jesus is placed in the sepulcher.

Was Jesus Still Wearing the Crown of Thorns along the Way to Calvary and on the Cross? We quote from the work of Msgr. Guilio Riccio.

"From the Gospels and from the historical context of the trial of Jesus, it is clear that the crowning with thorns went beyond Roman penal procedure and was simply a cruel joke thought up by the soldiers of the Praetorium to exalt, in their own way, the royalty that Jesus had shortly before asserted during his trial in front of Pilate. It was after the *'Ecce Homo!'* that is, when Pilate showed Jesus to the people, with the intention of demonstrating that he had been given an exemplary punishment, that Jesus appeared with the many marks of the scourging, dressed as a mock king with a purple mantle, and with a crown of thorns on His head. This crown must have made His face run with blood—that face which had already been beaten and punched, and made the target of spitting!

"Pilate's intention to free Jesus, expressed twice before the scourging, crumbled at the prospect of being involved in a charge of rebellion against the emperor: *'If you release him, you are not a Friend of Caesar'* (*Jn.* 19:12). Thus Pilate decreed death on the cross for Jesus. At this point the episode of the crown of thorns ends, since, when Jesus had to put His own clothes back on (*Mk.* 15:20) and be tied to the crosspiece for the painful journey, the bundle of thorns would have had to have been removed from His head.

"No reliable historical source would allow one to state that the crown of thorns was put back on Jesus' head again. The only sources which would suggest this derive from artistic representations, and these are several centuries after the event. Likewise, there is no evidence that it was removed and put on again after Jesus had been stripped of His clothes on Calvary. Furthermore, the tunic, which was made in one piece with an opening at the neck, probably could not have been put on or removed without first having removed the crown."

Riccio, Msgr Giulio. *The Way of the Cross in the Light of the Holy Shroud*, pp. 10-11.

Chapter 14

The Crucifixion and Death of Jesus

"And they came to a place called Golgotha (which means Place of the Skull)." The Latin name Calvary means scalp without hair or bald. Golgotha was a large skull-shaped rock rising about 45 feet above the ground. It was just outside the walls at the northern end of the city—an ideal spot for crucifixion, because it was elevated and near the city gates where many people passed.

There, they gave Jesus wine to drink mixed with gall. It was a Jewish custom to offer a narcotic to those about to be crucified to deaden the pain somewhat. *"But when Jesus tasted it, he refused the drink"* (*Mt.* 27:33-34). He wished to drink the cup of suffering in its fullness.

Then *"they crucified him"* (*Mk.*15:24). Those three words describe the most fearful torture in the ancient world. For those not doomed to death, no chastisement was greater than a scourging. As for those doomed to death, nothing was so horrific as crucifixion. Cicero called crucifixion "the most cruel and atrocious of punishments." The Romans always had a real dread for crucifixion.

The sequence of the crucifixion of Jesus and the two thieves was probably as follows: they stripped Jesus of His garments, crucified Him, and then the two thieves; then they nailed the inscriptions above the crosses, and divided the garments of the executed.

THE CRUCIFIXION

It was common among the Romans for a man to be nailed to the cross completely naked. But the Jews were very sen-

162

sitive on this point. So probably a cloth was wrapped around the loins of Jesus. Tradition says that Mary did this with her veil.

The crucified was made to lie on the ground with his shoulders on the crossbeam. His hands were extended and nailed to it. Then he was made to stand and was backed up to the vertical beam, which was about 15 to 20 feet high, so that the feet of the crucified would be on a level with a person's head.

The soldiers hoisted the person up by a rope fastened about his chest and thrown over the top of the vertical beam until he was able to straddle the *sedile*. The sedile was a small horn-shaped block halfway up the vertical beam, which the crucified was made to straddle to support the weight of his body.

The crosspiece was mortised to the vertical beam. Then the feet were nailed. According to the Shroud of Turin, the right foot was nailed to the beam, then the left foot was placed over the right and a nail driven through both the left and right foot.

St. Mark says, *"It was nine o'clock in the morning when they crucified him"* (15:25). St. John says that when Pilate pronounced the death sentence against Jesus, *"it was about noon"* (19:14). In our Lord's day, nine o'clock would be the beginning of the third hour (9:00 A.M. to noon) and noon would be the beginning of the sixth hour (noon to 3:00 P.M.). St. John's "about noon" could be about 11:30 A.M. and so within the third hour (9:00 A.M. to noon) mentioned by St. Mark.

THE TWO THIEVES

The gospel writers tell us *"two revolutionaries were crucified with Jesus one on his right and the other on his left"* (*Mt.* 27:38). The Greek word translated "revolutionaries" is the same word used to describe Barabbas. It can also mean robbers. According to the *Apocrypha* one thief was Dismas, the other Gesmas. They were crucified with Jesus in order to denigrate Him by association.

THE TITLE ON THE CROSS

When a man was put to death, the cause of his execution was written in red letters on a white board and affixed to the top of the cross. The inscription Pilate wrote to put on the cross for Jesus was INRI—"Jesus the Nazarean, the King of the Jews." It was written in Hebrew, the language of the natives; in Latin, the language of the Romans; and in Greek, the language of the learned (*Jn.* 19:19-20).

The inscription was Pilate's way of revenging himself on the Jewish leaders for their having forced him to crucify Jesus. The chief priests were quick to catch the implication. So they hurried to Pilate and said, "Don't write 'The King of the Jews,' but that he claimed to be the King of the Jews." Pilate had his moment of triumph. He answered, "What I have written, I have written."

JESUS' GARMENTS ARE DIVIDED

The clothing of an executed criminal went to his executioners. A Jew usually wore an outer robe, (*himation*), and beneath it a tunic, (*chiton*). Jesus' outer robe, girdle, sandals, and head-dress were divided among the four soldiers. But His tunic was seamless, like the tunic of the Jewish high priest, so the soldiers said, "Let's not tear it, but cast lots for it." In doing this, they fulfilled *Psalm* 21:19 (*Jn.* 19:23- 24). This seamless tunic is the theme of Stephen C. Douglas' historical novel *The Robe*.

THE SEVEN LAST WORDS

Jesus never ceased teaching. He did so to the very end of His life. His last words were few—only seven. The first three were for others: His enemies, a sinner, and us. The rest dealt with His relationship with His Father.

The first word: *"Father, forgive them, they know not what they do"* (*Lk.* 23-24).

Jesus prayed these words while they were nailing Him to the cross. He continued praying them as He looked out over the crowd taunting Him. Four classes of people were mocking Him. First, the passersby, *"You who would destroy the temple and rebuild it in three days, save yourself, if you are the Son of God, and come down from the cross!"* (*Mt.* 27:39-40). Then the chief priests and the scribes. Unlike the rabble, they did not direct their taunts at Jesus, rather they mockingly said to those around them, *"He saved others; he cannot save himself"* (*Mk.* 15:31). Thirdly, the robbers joined in the abuse. Finally, the soldiers jeered, calling out, *"If you are the King of the Jews, save yourself"* (*Lk.* 24:37).

But Jesus made no answer except to pray. And He did not save Himself, for it would not have benefited those who were requesting it.

The second word: *"Amen, I say to you, today you will be with me in Paradise"* (*Lk.* 23:43).

While the robbers were mocking Jesus, both were receiving great graces. They saw a man dying with love in His heart and forgiveness on His lips for those tormenting, jeering, and sneering at Him. The robber on the right, Dismas, responded to this grace. He prayed, "Jesus, remember me when You come into Your kingdom." The robber on the left, Gesmas, did not. He reviled Jesus, saying, "Save Yourself and us." Only to Dismas did Jesus say, "Amen, I say to you, today you will be with me in Paradise."

Dismas was converted in the last hour of his life to teach sinners never to despair—while there is life there is hope. But Gesmas did not convert to warn sinners never to presume on a deathbed conversion, but to work while it is still day. Dismas' salvation at the last moment teaches us to hope; Gesmas' obduracy in sin at death teaches us to avoid presumption.

The third word: *"Woman, behold, your son."* Then he said to the disciple, *"Behold, your mother"* (*Jn.* 19:26-27). *"Standing by the cross of Jesus were his mother and his mother's sister, Mary the wife of Clopas, and Mary of Magdala"* (*Jn.* 19:25). There has been much discussion as to whether this list names three or four women. I believe it names three, for "his mother's sister" very probably means "sister-in-law," for Hebrews called all close relatives "brothers" or "sisters." Mary's sister was her sister-in- law, Mary the wife of Clopas. Clopas or Alpheus was the brother of St. Joseph.

Mary was there at the foot of the cross. What pain her suffering caused Jesus; what pain His sufferings caused her! As any mother or father knows well by common human experience, the pain and suffering of their children weighs far more heavily on them than were they to suffer the same pain. Gathering what strength He could, He nodded to Mary and said, "Woman, behold, your son."

At the crib in Bethlehem, Mary became the Mother of Jesus. At the foot of the cross on Calvary, she became our mother—"Woman, behold your son." At the crib she brought forth her sinless Son with joy; on Calvary she brought forth us, her sinful children in pain.

> Nothing begins,nothing ends
> That is not paid with loan—
> For we are born in other's pain
> And perish in our own.

We cannot fathom the unspeakable pain that tore the heart of Mary as she must have asked herself, "How can I live without Him? How can I live with them—sinners?" Not to die with Him was great grief; but to have to live with us, that was a greater grief. But she did, for her last recorded words in Scriptures were, *"Do whatever He tells you."* So she became our mother, Mother of the Church. When He ascended into heaven, how she probably wanted to ascend with Him. But He willed otherwise. The Church needed her. The apostles needed her. We needed her. It was she who enabled the infant Church to grow. She held the apostles together. Once the Church had been fully established, on the eve of the first Council of the Church, the Council of Jerusalem, she returned to her Divine Son, A.D. 49. As harp strings burst asunder with the music they throb to express, so the heart of Mary broke with love and longing to behold her divine Son.

Then Jesus said to the beloved disciple, "Behold, your mother." Jesus' last gift to us was His greatest treasure: His Mother. "And from that hour the disciple took her into his home."

How wrong it is to deny Mary honor and devotion, as though such recognition would detract from the honor due Jesus. Such a denial would go contrary to the dying words of Jesus: "Behold your mother."

John Henry Cardinal Newman observed that those religious bodies that denied honor and devotion to Mary on the grounds that it detracted from the honor due to Christ eventually abandoned Christ. Whereas that religious body that honored Mary has remained faithful to Christ. It is a fact, the Mother always bring us to her Son.

Jesus addressed His Mother as "Woman." Only twice in John's gospel is Mary addressed by Jesus; and both times He calls her "Woman"—at Cana and here on Calvary. He did this to identify her with the woman in *Genesis* 3:15 whose offspring would crush the serpent's head and regain the paradise lost by the first Adam. He was the new Adam; she was the new Eve.

After having spoken His first three words, a long period of silence followed. In giving us His mother, He completed

His last will and testament. The day before, He had given His body and blood; now His mother.

Shel Silverstein has written a beautiful parable, *The Giving Tree*. It is a story of a tree that loved a little boy. Every day the boy came to the tree. He would eat her apples, swing from her branches, slide down her trunk, sleep in her shade . . . the tree was happy. But as the boy grew older, he began to want more and more from the tree, and the tree gave and gave and gave. And the tree was happy.

Jesus on the tree of the cross is like the giving tree. He loves us so much that He gives and gives and gives. He has given us Himself, His Mother, His flesh and blood—He has no more to give.

As if ashamed of man's ingratitude, darkness enshrouded the land when Jesus died on the tree of the cross. *"From noon onward, darkness came over the whole land until three in the afternoon" (Mt. 27:45)*. This darkness was very likely miraculous like the signs at the birth of Jesus. The darkness probably covered only the land of Judea.

During those three hours, Jesus simply endured the cross. Life is made up of action and passion, of doing and enduring. Often God asks us not so much to do things as to let things be done to us. He asked that of Mary at the Annunciation. He asked that of His Son on the cross. So with us, sometimes God asks us simply to bear our cross and to do nothing else. For the cross, when accepted, becomes redemptive like the sufferings of Jesus. His greatest work was not so much what He did, as what He let be done to Himself—His cross.

The fourth word: In reporting the execution of the Thane of Cawdor, William Shakespeare wrote: "Nothing in his life became him like the leaving it; he died as one that had been studied in his death" (Macbeth). Though Jesus lived as a carpenter's son, He died like a King! His first three words on the cross were spoken around twelve o'clock—all for others.

Then there was that darkness! It froze the spirit of His enemies. Silence enveloped them all. Jesus just hung there in excruciating torments. Near three o'clock the silence was shattered. Suddenly, in a loud voice, Jesus cried out, *"Eli, Eli, lema sabacthani?"* which means *"My God, my God, why have you forsaken me?"*

The Father could never forsake His Son. The union of the divine and the human in Jesus is indissoluble. "This word," wrote St. Leo the Great, "is not a complaint, but a lesson." Actually, these words are the beginning of *Psalm* 22. This Psalm predicts the sufferings of the Messiah. Jesus was applying it to Himself, and was thus affirming on the cross that He was the Messiah.

Some of the bystanders misunderstood. They took the words "'Eli, Eli," as referring to Elias. They thought pain had made Him delirious, asking the prophet to save Him. Actually, Jesus was praying the Messianic *Psalm* (22) which ends on a note of victory.

The fifth word: *"After this, aware that everything was now finished, in order that the scripture might be fulfilled, Jesus said, 'I thirst'"* (*Jn.* 19:28).

Thirst from loss of blood is quite natural. In the Civil War, wounded soldiers dying on the battlefield did not cry out, "My wound, my wounds!" No, they cried out, "Water! Water!" Loss of blood creates a burning thirst. St. John says this torment of Jesus fulfilled the prophecy of the Psalmist regarding the Messiah. *"My throat is dried up like baked clay, my tongue cleaves to my jaws"* (*Ps.* 22:16).

St. Augustine explained Jesus' fifth word this way: "I thirst to be thirsted for." In other words, His thirst was for souls. St. Francis once went through the streets of Assisi crying out, "Love is not loved!" How sad! We are like little children, picked up by adults to be hugged and kissed, but crying and kicking and shrieking, "Put me down." He asks for our love. So often we give Him gall; we do not slake His thirst.

At least one soldier was touched by His cry. He put a sponge soaked in wine on a sprig of hyssop and put it up to His mouth. Those who had been shouting about Elias did not like the soldier's action and tried to dissuade him, saying, *"Wait, let us see if Elijah comes to save him"* (*Mt.* 27:49). The soldier paid them no heed. (Scott Hahn says that this was the fourth cup that concluded the Last Supper, pg. 141-142).

The sixth word. Thus *"when Jesus had taken the wine, he said, 'It is finished'"* (*Jn.* 19:30). What is finished? The most useful life ever lived. What is finished? The fulfillment of all the prophecies concerning the Messiah. What is finished? The sacrifice of the New Covenant. What is finished? The work the Father had given Him to do—the redemption of the entire world. As all the works of creation were finished in six days, so in this sixth word, the work of salvation was finished: all men can now be saved, if they will. For as St. Augustine wrote: "He who created us without our consent will not save us without our consent."

The seventh word. Shortly afterward, Jesus again cried out in a loud voice, *"Father, into your hands I commend my spirit"* (*Lk.* 24:46). Here again Jesus was praying a *Psalm* (31:6). He cried out in a loud voice as proof of the freedom of His sacrifice: *"No one takes (my life) from me, but I lay it down on my own"* (*Jn.* 10:18).

"And bowing his head, he handed over the spirit" (*Jn.* 19:30). Death did not come to Him; if it had, He would have died first, then bowed His head. As it was, He bowed His head first; then death came as if at His nod. He was giving up His life; it was not being taken from Him—"Father, into Your hands I commend my spirit. And bowing His head, He died!" The Lamb of God died to take away the

sins of the world at 3:00 P.M., the very hour when the paschal lambs were being slain in the temple.

MIRACLES ACCOMPANYING THE DEATH OF JESUS

The veil before the Holy of Holies, which only the high priest could pass through once a year on the Day of Atonement, was torn in two from top to bottom. Dramatically, it said that now God is accessible to all.

Then the earth quaked and the rocks were split, tombs were opened and the bodies of many of the saints who had fallen asleep were raised. These events probably happened on Easter day when Jesus Himself arose from the dead.

When the Roman centurion in charge of the crucifixion saw all the strange happenings accompanying the death of Jesus and His incomparable dignity, he concluded that this man was truly the Son of God.

After Jesus had died, the chief priests and scribes headed for home to prepare for the Passover Feast. With no one to bully them, the crowd began to show their true feelings. They too returned to the city, but striking their breasts as if they had been party to some grave crime.

The holy women, however, stayed on at Golgotha. Some watched from a distance; some stood at the foot of the cross.

On the way home, the chief priests and scribes remembered that bodies should not hang on the cross on the Sabbath. The law commanded that the dead be buried before sunset (*Dt.* 21:23). So on their way home, they revisited Pilate and asked him to observe their law, suggesting at the same time that the simplest way to do this was to break the legs of those crucified, thus bringing on a quick death and making possible a quick burial. Pilate acceded.

The soldiers broke the legs of the two thieves, but when they came to Jesus, they found He was already dead.

However, to make sure, one soldier thrust his lance into His side and immediately blood and water flowed out.

That lance pierced two hearts: that of Jesus and that of Mary, fulfilling the prophecy of Simeon who had said, *"You yourself a sword shall pierce"* (*Lk.* 2:35). Tradition called this "lancer" Longinus, from the Greek word *lonche* meaning lance.

Longinus was probably from Anaxamum; this town's name was probably changed to Lanciano meaning "the lance." Here the first Eucharistic miracle took place around A.D. 700, in which the host changed to flesh and the wine to blood. Longinus' feast is on March 15. His statue is one of the four surrounding the high altar in St. Peter's Basilica in Rome.

Blood and water flowed from Jesus' pierced side. Physiologists presuppose Jesus' heart was literally broken before being pierced by the lance. When the heart is broken, the red globules sink to the bottom and the watery serum remains on top. When the pericardium is opened the two come out separately. Jesus' rapid death was due to a ruptured heart produced by mental suffering. Jesus died of a broken heart caused by grief.

Just before Jesus died, He had handed over His Spirit to His Church in the persons of Mary and John. Then when His side was pierced, the blood and the water that flowed from it symbolized the great sacraments that make the Church: the Holy Eucharist—the sacrament of love, and Baptism—the sacrament of cleansing from sin. Thus as from the side of the sleeping Adam came Eve, so from the side of the second Adam, asleep in death, came the new Eve, His Church.

While the soldiers were doing their cruel work, Joseph of Arimathea went to Pilate to obtain permission to bury Jesus and not have Him thrown into a common grave with criminals. Often great tragedy brings us to our senses. Joseph no longer worried what the rulers of the people might think, or what affect his siding with Jesus might have on his wealth. He saw what was the right thing to do and he did it regardless of the consequences. With Nicodemus and John, he took the body of Jesus down from the cross and laid it in the arms of His afflicted Mother.

When Mark Antony saw the body of Julius Caesar, covered with stab wounds, he muttered: "O pardon me, thou bleeding piece of earth,/ That I am meek and gentle with these butchers!" (Caesar's assassins). "Woe to the hand that shed this costly blood!/ Over thy wounds now do I prophesy,— . . . / A curse shall light upon the limbs of men/ Domestic fury and fierce civil strife/ Shall cumber all the parts of Italy;/ . . . and Caesar's spirit, ranging for revenge . . . / Shall with a monarch's voice/ Cry 'Havoc,' and let slip the dogs of war. . . ."

When Mary received the body of Jesus in her arms, there was no such spirit of revenge or rancor. She closed His mouth and shut His eyes; seeing the holes in hands and feet, the mangled flesh, the uncovered bones, she cried out, "Ah, Son, to what has Thy love for men brought Thee?" (St. Alphonsus, *The Glories of Mary,* p. 529).

Michelangelo in his masterpiece *"The Pieta"* has captured the spirit of Mary: it was one of total submission to the will of God and of suppressed sorrow at seeing what the sins of her children had done to her Son. But there was no rancor or bitterness of feeling.

Mary tried to fold the arms of Jesus, but she could not. Rigor mortis had set in, so His hands remained extended as if to invite all penitent sinners to return to Himself. "I asked Jesus, 'How much do you love me?' And Jesus said, 'This much . . . ' and He stretched out His arms and died."

No sinner should ever fear being rejected by Jesus. His

arms are extended to receive every penitent sinner who returns to Him. All one must do is to go to Him. But remember, He will be most easily found in the arms of Mary.

But Mary could not linger long in her contemplation; she had to hurry to bury Jesus, because the Sabbath was about to begin (*Lk.* 23:54). Joseph brought the linen cloth. Nicodemus brought about sixty pounds of spices. Again, time prevented them from carrying the body to a tomb any distance away. This problem was overcome by the generosity of Joseph who offered his own tomb nearby. Hewn out of rock, it could not be broken into. Since it was newly built for Joseph himself, there could be no mistaking that it was Jesus, and no one else, who emerged from it on Easter Sunday.

When Constantine built the Basilica of the Holy Sepulchre, the tomb was so close to Calvary that the Basilica could house them both. Thus in the one Basilica we can visit three places: Calvary, the stone of the anointing of the body of Jesus, and the tomb.

Jesus' burial was hasty to avoid breaking the Sabbath. When Alexander Hamilton was buried, the whole city of New York turned out. For Jesus' burial, there were only eight people. After Joseph and Nicodemus had *"rolled a huge stone across the entrance of the tomb, they departed"* (*Mt.* 27:60)— all departed but Mary Magdalene and the other Mary, wife of Clopas. They lingered behind to make sure of the spot where Jesus was laid, planning to come back after the Sabbath and complete the anointing done so hurriedly.

How bleak Saturday was for Mary! It was the first time earth was without her Son, for He had descended into Hell, not the hell of the dammed, but that other world where St. Joseph and all the saints of the Old Testament were awaiting Him. Her heart was empty, like the churches on Good Friday when the Blessed Sacrament is removed.

For the enemies of Jesus, however, the Passover must have been a most joyful one—their enemy was dead. Yet the more they thought of it, they remembered that Jesus had predicted that He would rise again on the third day. Of course they, especially the Sadducees, did not believe this; but they feared the disciples would come and steal the body and say that He had risen from the dead.

So on Saturday they made the short walk, (legitimate on that day), to Pilate and asked that the tomb be sealed and guarded until the third day. The seal would make sure that the soldiers could not be bribed into letting the disciples into the tomb to steal the body. The ways of God are wondrous indeed: these extraordinary precautions only served to make the reality of the resurrection of Jesus on Easter Sunday all the more certain.

Chapter 15

The Resurrection of Jesus

One of the astounding facts about the resurrection of Jesus is that His enemies were inclined to believe it, whereas His friends didn't even think of it! His enemies sealed the tomb and put guards around it. His friends, the holy women, came to the tomb on the first day of the week only to anoint the body of Jesus. The Jewish day was reckoned from sunset to sunset. Jesus was in the tomb part of Friday, the whole of Saturday and part of Sunday; thus three days, and two nights, or about forty hours.

When the Sabbath was over, that is, after six o'clock Saturday evening, April 8, Mary Magdalene, Mary the wife of Clopas, Salome, the mother of the sons of Zebedee, and Joanna, the wife of Chusa, Herod's steward, bought spices to anoint the body of Jesus (*Mk.* 16:1).

So, very early Sunday morning, while it was still dark, the holy women hurried to the tomb in silence. As the light began to dawn and people started to appear on the streets, the women asked each other, "Who will roll back the stone for us from the entrance to the tomb?" Apparently, they were unaware that guards had been posted at the tomb on Saturday night.

Still they went—stone or no stone. As they were passing through the city gate leading to Golgotha, an angel from Heaven solved the stone problem; he took the huge millstone at the entrance of the tomb, picked it up and slammed it to the ground with such force that the earth quaked. He sat upon it. His appearance was like lightning; his garments, white as snow. He terrified the guards, who fled to the city. Thus in one fell swoop, God removed all obstacles for the holy women. Often, anticipated problems cause us to give up enterprises of great pith and moment only to discover that had we persevered, the problem would not be there, as for the holy women.

In their flight, the guards suddenly realized that they had deserted their post. For a Roman soldier that meant death. So they had recourse to the chief priests. They told their story. Far from responding to this grace, the priests consulted within themselves and decided to bribe the soldiers into saying that the friends of Jesus had stolen His body while they were asleep. As for their desertion, they promised to make it right for them with Pilate.

The guards took the money and peddled the lie that the disciples of Jesus stole His body while they were asleep—a lie which, according to St. Matthew, persisted even to his day. Once again, Jesus was betrayed for money. St. Augustine torpedoed their lie when he said, "Of what avail are sleeping witnesses?"

The exact time Jesus rose from the dead is unknown. Probably it occurred during the early hours of Sunday morning. No one witnessed it. Our Lord arose and passed through the stone at the entrance of the tomb just as He would pass through the doors of the Upper Room that same Sunday evening.

When the women heard the earth quake near the tomb, Mary Magdalene probably hurried on ahead, for love is impetuous. She saw the stone flat on the ground, the tomb wide opened, and jumped to the conclusion that someone had violated the grave. She scooted off to tell Peter and John about the empty tomb.

While she was on her way, the other women arrived at the tomb. An angel sitting on the tombstone said to them,

"Fear not!" He escorted them into the tomb. There, another angel appeared who also told them not to fear. Then two angels in dazzling garments stood on each side of them and told them to go and tell Peter and the other disciples that Jesus was risen and would go before them into Galilee. Jesus chose Galilee because Jerusalem was a place of terror for His disciples. Already Joseph of Arimathea had probably been arrested. But in remote Galilee, the power of the Sanhedrin was less strong. Most of His followers were from Galilee—they would feel more secure and freer there. But more important, Jesus was weaning them from Jerusalem, because He intended the center of His Church to be elsewhere.

At first the women left the tomb dumbstruck; they were afraid and said nothing. When they had overcome their fear, they departed quickly and reported to the Eleven and the rest all that the angels had told them. Their story was branded as women's idle talk.

Meanwhile, Mary Magdalene, Peter and John were racing off to the tomb. Peter and John found it just as Mary had said. But when they saw the burial linens neatly wrapped up, they knew that no one had stolen the body, as Mary Magdalene had surmised. They left deep in thought to talk things over with the others.

Mary Magdalene, however, stayed on behind weeping. Jesus approached her, but she mistook Him for the gardener. There must have been something distinctly wonderful about His voice, because when He said to her, *"Mary!"* she recognized Him at once. Oh, with what profound joy and love, she cried out, *"Rabboni,"* which means "My Teacher"! She embraced His feet as if she would never let Him go again. Jesus gently raised her up; and, with His usual concern for others, He told her to go to His disciples and tell them the good news. She went and how she must have burst out to them, "I have seen the Lord!"

Though Jesus' appearance to Mary Magdalene is the first recorded in the Gospel, tradition testifies that His very first appearance was probably to His sorrowing Mother at the very moment of His resurrection. The Church acknowledges this tradition by making the principal church of our Blessed Mother, St. Mary Major, the station Church for Easter Sunday.

Also the hymn *Regina Coeli,* affirms this tradition. Instead of the *Angelus,* during the Easter season the *Regina Coeli* is prayed. On that first Easter Sunday morn, Gabriel came to Mary and said, "O Queen of Heaven, rejoice, alleluia. He whom thou didst merit to bear, alleluia. Has risen as He said, alleluia. Rejoice and be glad, O Virgin Mary, alleluia! For the Lord has truly risen, alleluia."

APPEARANCE TO THE TWO DISCIPLES ON THE WAY TO EMMAUS

Pilgrims did not have to stay in Jerusalem for the eight days of the Passover. On the day after the Pasch, many set out for home. This was what two disciples of Jesus did. One was named Cleopas. Depressed and disappointed, they set out about nine in the morning for their home village of Emmaus, seven miles west of Jerusalem. The fact that they were heading home and not for Galilee showed how little stock they had put in the women's story about the empty tomb and the angels.

It was the third day. Evidently, they had waited to see— but not for the full three days. So often God gives His graces at the last moment, as He did when Abraham was about to sacrifice his son Isaac. On Easter, the third day, Jesus actually appeared to the disciples, but at the end of the day.

The two had not waited long enough. Jesus had two things more to do to finish the founding of His Church before returning to the Father: one was to give her the power to forgive sins; the other was to give her a head, to name His successor, His vicar on earth.

In giving the Church the power to forgive sins, He wanted all His disciples to be present, so He revealed Himself to the two disciples of Emmaus. He did this at the breaking of the bread, as if to teach them that His presence with them from now on would be a sacramental one. When they recognized Him, they were so elated, they took horses and sped back to Jerusalem. They arrived there about eight or nine in the evening. Before they could tell their story to the others, the disciples excitedly told them that Jesus had appeared to Simon Peter, probably that Sunday afternoon. Only then were they able to recount their story (*Lk.* 24:13- 32).

While they were telling it, Jesus stood in their midst, even though the doors were locked. The room was probably the Upper Room in the house of John Mark, who wrote the gospel of Mark. Jesus said to them, "Peace be with you." Then He instituted the Sacrament of Reconciliation (*Jn.* 20:21-23). Jesus' redemption was His great act of mercy; He wished the power to forgive sins to be the great sacrament of His mercy.

To Blessed Mary Faustina, Jesus said: "In the Tribunal of Mercy (the sacrament of Reconciliation) . . . the greatest miracles take place . . . Here the misery of the soul meets the God of mercy . . . I Myself am waiting there for you. I am only hidden by the priest . . . The person of the priest is, for Me, only a screen . . . ."

These six appearances of Jesus occurred in Jerusalem on Easter Sunday. (See Note at end of chapter.)

The apostles probably stayed in Jerusalem for the entire octave of the Passover which ended on Friday. The next day being the Sabbath, they could not leave Jerusalem. We don't know exactly what kept them there on the next day,

Sunday, April 16. Perhaps they were already learning to keep the Sunday holy because Jesus had arisen from the dead on Sunday and had first appeared to them on Sunday. In any event, they were still there on Sunday in the Upper Room and on this occasion Thomas was with them. The apostles had been telling him all week long that they had seen the risen Lord and His wounds. Thomas protested that he would not believe this until he saw for himself. But just to make sure, Thomas stayed with the others.

Graciously, Jesus accommodated the doubter on this Sunday. The doors again were closed, but Jesus came through them. He singled out Thomas. The fact that Jesus showed He was fully aware of Thomas' doubt was enough to convince him. The doubter dropped to his knees and confessed, "My Lord and my God!"

After these things, Jesus left Jerusalem for Galilee. There, away from Jerusalem, He planned to conclude the founding of His Church by giving her a head to succeed Himself, to take His place. So He walked by the Sea of Galilee and appeared to seven disciples. They had been fishing all night but had caught nothing. In the early morning Jesus bade them to cast their net on the right side of the boat. They did and the haul of fish was so great they had trouble dragging it to shore. Without Jesus we can do nothing; with Jesus there is nothing we cannot do.

The clean-hearted John was the first to recognize Jesus. He said to Peter, "It is the Lord." When Peter heard this, he, with his usual impetuosity and tremendous loving heart, jumped into the sea. Jesus had made breakfast for them.

After they had breakfasted, and Jesus had seen to it that all had had their fill, He did not vanish as He had been accustomed to doing during these forty days. He lingered on, for He had something very important to do.

He looked at Peter, straight in the face with a look of

love, not one of condemnation for his denials, and He said, "Simon, son of John, do you love me more than these?" It was like starting all over again by calling him "Simon, son of John." In spite of all his past failures, Simon knew he loved Jesus. With his usual fervor and impetuousness, he answered, "Lord, you know that I love you."

Jesus waited. All the disciples were silent. They felt this was a vital moment in their lives, as well as in the life of Simon. Slowly, Jesus said, "Feed my lambs." All understood at once that Jesus was reinstating Simon in the office promised him at Caesarea-Philippi. There could be no doubt. The one who feeds the lambs is the shepherd.

After a pause, Jesus spoke again, weighing each word He uttered. "Simon, son of John, do you love me?" Before, He had made a comparison—"love me more than these." Now He asked Simon to study his own heart. "Do you love me?"

What could Simon say more than what he had already said. "Lord, you know I love you." Jesus said, "Tend my sheep." It was a promotion. The shepherd was not only to feed, but to guide and rule the flock. All the disciples realized now that Jesus was giving Simon the power of the keys.

A third time Jesus spoke. Now, He asked Simon, "Do you love me?" At first Peter did not grasp the steps by which Jesus was restoring him to honor. All that he knew was that He loved Jesus and loved Him intensely, even more than his very self. The repetitious questions of Jesus distressed Peter; they seemed to cast doubt upon his confession. What could he say? He appealed to Jesus Himself. "Lord, you know everything; you know that I love you." Joyfully, Jesus accepted his confession. "Feed my sheep."

The three denials of Peter had been expiated by three acts of love, and Peter was elevated beyond all his expectations. He was to take the place of the Good Shepherd, to be His vicar on earth: to feed, to tend, to guide, to rule the lambs and the sheep, the laity and the hierarchy. And like the Good Shepherd, he too would lay down his life for the sheep—"when you grow old, you will stretch out your hands." And Peter did: he was crucified during the reign of Nero (54-68) according to Tertullian (ca. 225). The historian Eusebius (ca. 339) adds, on the authority of Origen (d. 253), that by his own desire he suffered head downward on Vatican hill.

The last step in the founding of His Church was now complete. Jesus had a vicar on earth—one to take His place; one to head His Church and give her the unity that would be the mark that she was the true Church, His Church. And since this power was given for the good of the flock, Jesus meant it to last as long as the flock itself. He meant this power to be passed on not only to Peter, but to his successors.

Near the end of forty days, Jesus returned to Jerusalem. His final appearance was in the Upper Room. After giving Holy Communion to the disciples, He led them toward Bethany, to the Mount of Olives. Near the top of the Mount, in sight of Jerusalem, He commissioned His apostles to go and make disciples of all nations (*Mt.* 28:16-20).

His work was done; now it was time for the Church to carry on His work. However, before she could, there remained only one final and all-important gift He had to give Her: the Holy Spirit. So promising to send them the Holy Spirit, He blessed them and ascended into Heaven (*Acts* 1:8-10). It was a Thursday, May 18, A.D. 30, probably at noon.

To mark the spot of the Ascension, a round structure was built in A.D. 380 encircling the "Rock of the Ascension," which is said to contain Christ's footprint. Originally the chapel had no dome. In 1187 the Moslems took the shrine and covered it with a dome, which incidentally became the main inspiration for the Dome of the Rock Mosque in Jerusalem.

Jesus died when the day was ending; He rose when the day was beginning; and He ascended into Heaven when it was midday (*Ps.* 55:18).

With the Ascension the life of Jesus ended and the life of the Church began: the Messianic era which is to last to the end of the world.

Just before ascending into Heaven, Jesus said to His disciples: *"You will receive power when the Holy Spirit comes upon you, and you will be my witnesses in Jerusalem, throughout Judea and Samaria, and the ends of the earth"* (*Acts* 1:8). Then He was lifted up.

The disciples returned to Jerusalem to the upper room; they consisted of the apostles, some women, and "Mary the mother of Jesus, and his brothers (brethren)." For nine days they prayed, making the first novena. In answer to those powerful prayers, offered with Mary, the Holy Spirit came down upon them all with a noise like a strong driving wind. Tongues of fire appeared, parted and rested on each of them; and they were filled with the Holy Spirit and began to speak in different tongues.

The Spirit filled the apostles with courage and with knowledge. He illuminated their minds regarding Jesus and all that He had taught them; and He empowered them to proclaim courageously, clearly and fearlessly the good news of the resurrection of Jesus. They went forth from the upper room and did exactly as Jesus had commanded them: they preached and they baptized. They understood what Jesus had meant when He said to Peter, "Feed my sheep," and they deferred to him. Peter spoke for them all on that first Pentecost Sunday and "about three thousand persons were added that day" to the disciples of Jesus. The Church was born.

For Mary, however, the Spirit came to fill her with a new love, a love like that for her Son, but now for the Church and for all of us who were committed to her by Jesus from the cross. The Spirit filled her with such love that she could truly become "Mother of the Church." During those early, trying days of the Church, it was Mary who guided the apostles, kept them loyal to her Son and inspired them to teach all nations.

The Church is interested in the same goal as was Jesus: the salvation of all the world. Its ultimate reason for existing is the Glory of God Himself.

William Gladstone in a speech against the law excluding Catholics from the Lord Chancellorship of England said:

"The Catholic Church has marched for 1500 years at the head of civilization. Her greatness, glory, grandeur and majesty have been almost, though not absolutely, all that in these respects the world has had to boast of. Her children are more numerous than all the members of the sects combined. Her altars are raised in every clime and her missionaries are wherever there are souls to be saved.

"And this wondrous Church, as old as Christianity, as universal as mankind, is today, after twenty centuries, as fresh, as vigorous and as faithful as on the day when the Pentecostal fires were showered upon the earth."

* * *

Note

The appearances of Jesus after His resurrection were as follows:

1. To the Blessed Virgin Mary.
2. To Mary Magdalene.
3. To the other women.
4. To Peter on Easter Sunday afternoon.
5. To the two disciples on the way to Emmaus.
6. To the Apostles (except Thomas). These six appearances occurred on Easter Sunday.

7. To the Apostles including Thomas, a week later.
8. In Galilee near the Lake of Gennesareth, to seven disciples.
9. On a mountain in Galilee to a multitude of disciples.
10. To James (1 Cor. 15:7).
11. The final appearance was at the Ascension (Acts 1:9-10).

St. Leo the Great wrote: "Throughout the whole period between the resurrection and the ascension, God's providence was at work to instill this one lesson into the hearts of the disciples, to set this one truth before their eyes, that our Lord Jesus Christ, who was truly born, truly suffered, and truly died, should be recognized as truly risen from the dead" *(Sermon on the Ascension).*

Appendix

Chronology of the Life of Jesus According to Best Exegetes

35-25 B.C.	Birth of Joseph
21-20 B.C.	Birth of Mary
7 B.C.	Betrothal of Mary and Joseph
Sept., 6 B.C.	Birth of Jesus
A.D. 15	Death of Joseph

Public Life of Jesus

Oct. A.D. 27	Preaching of John the Baptist
Jan. A.D. 28	Baptism of Jesus
Feb. A.D. 28	Temptations of Jesus
March A.D. 28	Wedding Feast at Cana
March 30, A.D. 28	**First Passover**
April A.D. 28	Nicodemus
May A.D. 28	Samaritan woman
	Galilean ministry (south)
June A.D. 28	Galilean ministry (north)
	Call of Matthew
	Conflicts with Pharisees
July A.D. 28	Sermon on the Mount
Aug.-Sept. A.D. 28	Testimony of John, Magdalene
Oct. A.D. 28	Tours Galilee
Nov. A.D. 28	Parables on the kingdom
Dec. A.D. 28	Raises Jairus' daughter
	Second visit to Nazareth
Jan.-March A.D. 29	Tours towns and villages of Galilee

March-April A.D. 29	Mission of 12
	Martyrdom of John the Baptist
	Promise of the Eucharist
April 18, A.D. 29	**Second Passover**
May-June A.D. 29	Tours Syro-Phoenicia
July A.D. 29	Peter's confession of faith
August A.D. 29	Transfiguration
Sept. A.D. 29	Leaves Galilee
	Condemns the sinful cities
Oct. A.D. 29	Feast of Tabernacles
Nov.-Dec. A.D. 29	Judean ministry
Dec. A.D. 29	Feast of Dedication
Jan.-April A.D. 30	Perean Ministry
April 2, A.D. 30	Entry into Jerusalem (Palm Sunday)
April 6, A.D. 30	Holy Thursday
April 7, A.D. 30	**Third Passover (Good Friday)**
April 9, A.D. 30	Resurrection (Easter Sunday)
May 18, A.D. 30	Ascension